DON'T SING
ANY SAD
SONGS

*A Down Syndrome Daughter's
Joyful Journey*

Rosalie B. Icenhower

AmErica House
Baltimore

Copyright 2000 by Rosalie B. Icenhower

First printing

ISBN: 1-893162-83-4

PUBLISHED BY AMERICA HOUSE BOOK PUBLISHERS
www.publishamerica.com
Baltimore

Printed in the United States of America

To all whose dreams have been shattered by the birth of a less-than-perfect child:
May our Lord use Becky's story to give you hope, encouragement, and "...songs in the night with grace to sing them anywhere."

Preface

Don't Sing Any Sad Songs is not a "how-to" book of prescriptions. Many other competent authors have already written about the diagnosis, cause, care, training, and education of people with Down syndrome.

This is simply the story of one delightful Down syndrome woman, our daughter, Becky, who moved away from home as a young adult, and lives a loving, joy-filled, productive life.

Becky is not a savant, an angel, nor a pet. She is a daughter of our Heavenly Father -- and if she ever meets you, she will claim you as her friend.

June, 1999
Rosalie B. Icenhower

DON'T SING ANY SAD SONGS

A Note to Readers

The term, "mongoloid," is used in specific quotations in this book. That was a term used through the 1960's and then replaced by "Down syndrome." Currently there are many "politically correct" terms, such as "differently abled," "developmentally delayed," and others now in use that change from year to year.

Note also that sentences containing direct quotations attributed to Becky often leave out verbs, mostly "be" verbs: *am, are, is, was, were, have, has, had.* These sentences are typical of her speech patterns. Thus, if she says, "I cold," the hearer or reader must "supply" the missing verb. Generally it is quite clearly understood in context whether the verb is past, present, or future tense. Occasionally, she also drops the final "ed" in past tense verbs.

DON'T SING ANY SAD SONGS

Introduction

Perhaps I cannot speak for those parents experiencing a different, harsher journey than ours with our Down syndrome daughter. My prayer is that our story will show them this: just as no one can judge the quality of a musical score by its first note alone, neither can one successfully predict what a child at birth will become in later years.

Several times in the last couple of years after I've spoken to a women's group, one or two ladies have approached me, confiding that they are either pregnant with or have recently given birth to a baby with special needs. They want to know more about my daughter Becky, how I cope with particular problems, how well others accept her, and my advice in rearing their children.

With new technologies developed in the early 1960's, testing of pre-born children began in earnest. A segment of the population appeared to be doomed as an "endangered species" when abortion on demand was legalized in 1973, especially those with Down syndrome or other abnormal intellectual or physical impairments.

Lately, it seems, nearly every expectant parent we meet has ultrasound pictures of the unborn offspring to pass around for everyone to see. From time to time mothers-to-be *(especially in their late 30's-early 40's)* tell us their doctors ask if they also want amniocentesis *(testing of the amniotic fluid surrounding the fetus)* or genetic blood tests to detect anomalies not picked up by ultrasound.

Mentally and physically disabled persons are *not* a small minority. In the United States, 48.9 million persons have some sort of handicap. Approximately 14.7 million Americans of working age have a "severe disability," according to the President's Committee on Employment of

People With Disabilities. One or two of every 1,000 babies conceived in the U.S. has Down syndrome. The percentages increase with the age of the mothers; this is why amniocentesis is suggested for those over a certain age.

Yet, at the dawning of the new millennium, something new is in the air. Expectant parents, learning that their baby will have special problems, are opting *not* to abort but to give birth -- beginning an admittedly more challenging journey into parenthood. Dr. Bern Alberda, a Seattle pediatrician, recently told me a young couple asked about their chances for adopting a special needs child. Shortly after their inquiry, the woman became pregnant and the couple gave birth to a Down syndrome baby of their own.

"They're doing a wonderful job of parenting," the doctor told me. God had already prepared their hearts to welcome this child.

There is a new openness these days. Books, newspaper and magazine articles feature celebrity parents, such as actress Julie Newmar, whose son has Down syndrome. Well-known football coach, Gene Stallings, has written about his Down syndrome son, John Mark. Steve Largent, a Hall of Fame football star, currently a U. S. congressman representing Oklahoma, has a son, Kramer, with spina bifida.

Visibility and encouragement have replaced myths, misunderstanding, and embarrassment. I pray that fifty years from now medical research leading to miracles, performed *in utero*, will be common. Then indeed there will be "no sad songs" sung for any of the John Marks, Kramers, Beckys, and their families.

But this is not a medical book nor a philosophical treatise on moral or Christian ethics. Rather, it is a story how a delightful person named Becky taught a not-so-famous family to sing joyous praise to God, not dirges, as one would expect us to sing when the youngest member of the clan has a measured I.Q. of 36!

Becky lights up a room with pure sunshine when she enters. One can no more be depressed in her presence than a car can fly to the moon. She has changed my own life dramatically in terms of dependence upon our Heavenly Father and in redirecting many of my own goals. Because of her, I went to college and graduate schools, enabling me to minister to hundreds of people I could not have touched otherwise.

Her presence in the family taught her sister and two brothers patience, understanding, compassion, and love for differently abled people. No doubt exists in our family that we are far better people, all of us, than we would have been without her.

We've found that it is not true that "God gives special children to special people;" He *does* give grace! May it be that through Becky's story many other families will find hope and encouragement *(and their own joyful songs)* for the road ahead.

13

DON'T SING ANY SAD SONGS

Prologue

"The Special Child"

I never would have chosen you,
O child of mine, little bird
With broken wing:
I'd have chosen a brighter bird
Who could rise on wings of praise
To sing to God.

But God, in His infinite care,
Chose you for me, little girl,
To strengthen me.
You have taught me greater love:
My heart is a richer place
Because you came.

I never would have chosen you,
But our God has chosen me
To care for you.
I'd have chosen a perfect child--
And I'd never have known the joy
You've brought to me.

*Note: My original poems on pages 6, 36, and 83,   are reprinted by permission of **The Banner**. Scripture taken from the HOLY BIBLE, NEW INTERNATIONAL VERSION, Used by permission of Zondervan Bible Publishers.*

DON'T SING ANY SAD SONGS

Chapter 1
A Sad Song Begins

Among the many songs I may have wanted to sing in 1964, I wouldn't have chosen a fourth lullaby quite so soon. My husband Paul and I already had three little ones under four years old; the third one, David, arrived on New Year's Eve, 1962. But I became pregnant again four months later.

"How in the world," I muttered, "am I going to work another baby into my schedule just now? My day is more than full and running over already."

Keeping up with the three children we already had was nearly overwhelming to me.

Debbie, our first-born, had been diagnosed with Juvenile Rheumatoid Arthritis soon after she turned three. Within a year, she had gone from a plump, bright-eyed toddler to a thin, pale "little old lady" in a matter of months. Her wrists, knees, and neck were particularly affected. As a result, she was unable to even partially pull on her socks or perform many other ordinary self-help tasks most children that age can accomplish. Because she stubbornly resisted help, I had to watch for silent signals that her pain was severe. Only when she rubbed her eyes to keep tears from rolling down her cheeks, could I give assistance to my "Little Miss Independence."

Quite probably David would still in be in diapers and not walking yet when the new child arrived. Jonathan was not naughty, just energetic, a natural explorer. Long before he was three, he'd already climbed to the top of the loquat tree that was higher than our house. So to say that I was singing with angelic joy about having four babies in less than four years is a gross understatement. In fact, I was angry with God for several weeks.

My own sad song, "Poor, Poor Me," droned monotonously on and on. One would think I was trapped in a gloomy prison where I could see nothing beyond the bars! Actually, I loved being a mom, but not to one baby after the other in such quick succession. Even if abortion had been a legal option at that time, neither Paul nor I would have considered such a thing for a moment. I merely needed to vent my personal frustration.

"Look," I said, "I still have two or three loads of laundry every day, plus the house to keep clean, meals to prepare, articles and news to write."

I was going out nearly every night to City Council or some other civic meeting, covering my beat as a daily newspaper correspondent.

We desperately needed every penny of that additional income. Our greatest concern was having enough money to pay Debbie's astronomical medical bills, not covered by our insurance. "Honey," I asked my husband, "how in the world will we get along without my job? I can't possibly handle another baby and this job, too!"

I usually got to bed at 2:00 A.M. after writing my news stories, and got up again at 6:00 to take care of David, who always woke up early. My daily goal: the children dressed and fed, breakfast dishes done, floors vacuumed, furniture dusted, beds made, two loads of laundry done, folded, and put away by 10:00 A.M.

Menus were planned a week ahead of time, so I knew exactly how much time to allot for meal preparation. So after all *that* was done, I had the rest of the day to sit on the floor, play, read, and sing with the children. About once a week we either had other teachers' wives and children over for coffee, or we went to one of their homes. *(Yes, now I become exhausted just remembering all that I used to do!)*

"My calling in life," I joked with friends, "is to keep on producing beautiful, intelligent children and still be completely organized."

Much as I complained about my frenzied schedule, it kept me from expressing concern about the soft, small kicks within my womb. Surely everything would go well with this baby's development and delivery. Hadn't it always?

"This one feels like a small butterfly," I told Paul. "Instead of the good, strong kicks the boys gave, this one gives me a gentle pat now and then. Other times, it feels like there's a little butterfly doing a tap dance. Must be another girl!"

What happened on January 3 certainly was not part of my carefully orchestrated schedule. Shortly after sunrise I awoke with a start, feeling a wet bed beneath me.

"Oh, no!" I moaned, waking Paul. "I think my water just broke! But how can that be? The baby isn't due for another six weeks. It's coming too early. Just what I don't need!"

But it wasn't water at all; it was blood. I was hemorrhaging. My doctor instructed us to come to the hospital, seven miles away, as quickly as possible. We left in minutes, even before our near-by sitter could climb our front steps.

Dr. Veldstra was clearly concerned: "This is *placenta previa*, Rosalie, not normal labor. We have to get this bleeding under control, and I mean *now*."

He explained that *placenta previa* is the medical term for partial detachment of the placenta from the uterus late in

19

pregnancy. Both the mother and child's lives are jeopardized if the bleeding cannot be controlled.

"We don't want the baby to come yet," he said, shaking his head. "Six weeks early is too soon for this one. It's not nearly big enough."

The doctor gave me injections to stop the bleeding and the labor contractions that had begun. They would slow down, then suddenly pick up in frequency and intensity.

Paul stayed at my bedside all day, fervently praying for our child's life. At one point, my doctor called in a consultant who informed us that unless the bleeding stopped within fifteen minutes, the baby would have to be taken by C-section in order to save my life, as well as the baby's. God heard our prayers; the bleeding subsided. Falling into exhausted sleep, I was confident of His merciful care.

"No pillow under your head, young lady, nor will you sit up or turn over, for the next six weeks. Doctor's orders, you know," Olee Baker, the hospital's obstetrics nurse reminded me three days later, when I was allowed to go home by ambulance.

Lessons in patience and thanksgiving were about to begin, despite my Litany of Grouse: "Six weeks in bed? Just what I don't need! Three kids to take care of, news events to cover..."

Had we not lived in Ripon, California, I'm not sure any of our household could have survived those next weeks. This small city in the fertile San Joaquin Valley boasts it is "The Almond Capital of the World." More impressively, Ripon cares for its own.

In the 1960's the area was still largely made up of first and second generation Dutch immigrants. Nearly all our friends were hard-working, thrifty, conscientious Christians, as solid in their loyalties as in their muscular frames. Not given to lengthy, emotional testimonies, they demonstrated their living faith in very practical ways.

Dorothy DeJong and Wolena Smink alternated days in coming to bathe me and change the bed. Dorothy, a Registered Nurse, took David home with her, though she had six children of her own. Neighbors scheduled themselves to care for Debbie and Jonathan and keep the house clean. Still others brought dinner each day.

Through my tears I asked, "How can we ever repay all of you for doing so much?"

Wolena replied, "Probably you'll never repay *us*, but you can pass the blessing on by helping others when you're able."

Paul had a phone installed next to my bed so I could continue to do my news reporting by contacting my sources, and phoning the stories in to the newspaper. *(There weren't any fax machines or personal computers with modems then, remember?)*

Each day crawled by like a drugged turtle. Friends kindly offered me books and magazines to read. Do you know it's an impossibility to read while lying absolutely flat? I soon found that my arms ached if I held even the slimmest magazine for a few minutes. While others said they envied my prolonged "vacation," I knew they wouldn't trade places!

I longed to cuddle and rock my babies, play and sing with them. Paul and I had had an early Saturday morning ritual of piling the kids onto our bed to play, tickle, and sing

21

before we got up. Now Debbie and Jonathan couldn't understand why they couldn't climb into bed with me. And it nearly broke my heart when Dorothy brought David to see me several times--he clung to her and called her "Mama."

February 16, our baby's due date, arrived at last. Right on schedule, my contractions began. We drove off to the hospital rejoicing that the long ordeal was nearly over.

Things seemed to be going along well, when Nurse Baker came to check me for the umpteenth time. She moved a cold stethoscope here and there over my extended tummy. Without a word, she turned and ran down the hospital corridor. Breathlessly, she came running back in a matter of seconds, the doctor following at a brisk pace.

He checked me and said, "We're going into the delivery room right now."

"But I'm not ready!" I protested. I was positive my body was not signaling the baby to come just yet.

As I was being draped in the delivery room, the doctor told me, "We're going to pull the baby out right now."

Unceremoniously, my feet were placed in the stirrups. For some reason I did not expect such searing pain. I'd had no need nor desire for anesthesia for my first two deliveries, and had asked for only minimal relief for David's birth. Now pain zigzagged like lightning from my abdomen to my shoulders as the doctor and nurses went to work.

Truthfully, I was more than a bit miffed. These people didn't seem to care one speck what I might think of this barbaric procedure! Somehow I was under the

22

impression the doctor was hurrying me along so he could take care of another patient.

"If they'd allowed me a few more minutes, I'd have given a couple good pushes and had the baby! Why do they think they have to pull the baby out, anyway? Just because I'm not a groaner nor a screamer doesn't mean this is a picnic!" I muttered under my breath. "This isn't fair to me or to the baby."

Time worked in slow motion. After what seemed like hours, someone pushed a mask over my nose and mouth, saying, "Take a few deep breaths, please."

"No," I said, pulling away as best I could, "if I couldn't have anything for pain when I needed it, I don't want it now." At that moment, I felt just plain stubborn.

"This is oxygen, and it's for the baby's sake," the doctor answered.

I stopped struggling and gulped a couple of big breaths.

After a few more minutes, Dr. Veldstra said, "You have a little girl, Rosalie."

"Good! Her name is Rebecca," I said, too tired to ask details. "Is she okay?"

"We're giving you something to help you sleep for awhile," the doctor said.

I drifted in and out of a hazy cloud. Not sure at times whether I was awake or dreaming, I continued to ask, "Is my baby all right?"

Finally, I distinctly heard a soft cry, and the doctor saying, "Yes, Rosalie, she's okay." But his voice sounded weary and flat.

When I awoke back in my room, Paul was standing at my bedside, stroking my hair. He bent down and kissed me.

"How are you, honey?" he asked. "You've been talking in your sleep, and you seemed pretty agitated about something."

I told him how frustrated I was with the doctor: "I can't figure out why he was in such a hurry. I think he had another patient. And they hurried the baby away so fast, I hardly got a glimpse of her."

"Honey," Paul said quietly, "Becky's heart had stopped, and the doctor had to deliver her right away. He had no choice. There wasn't time for a C-section. We very nearly lost her."

The same hazy cloud enveloped my entire being again. Now grateful for Dr. Veldstra's quick action, I drifted off to sleep.

Our newborn had been popped into an Isolette after her delivery, so I didn't get a good look at her until the next morning. When a nurse laid her in my arms, I turned down the pink wrapper, expecting to see a red-faced infant looking much like our other babies did at birth. Instead, I saw a tiny face with a mottled blue and yellow complexion.

"She's a little jaundiced, like many babies are," the young nurse explained as she left. "And she's still a tad bit cold. I'll come and get her and put her back in the Isolette to warm her up in just a few minutes."

But it wasn't the unnatural color that upset me, though I'd have been more concerned had I fully realized she was still having some breathing problems. It was her slanted eyes, the flared nares of her button-sized nose, the wobbly neck that sickened me. Immediately I'd recognized

24

these as common Down syndrome features. I felt as though someone had struck my stomach with a sledgehammer.

"Oh, Lord God!" I cried out to my Heavenly Father. "Why me? Why *me*? What are You doing to me!"

Then I laughed aloud and said, "Why *not* me, Father?"

I realized how utterly arrogant it was for me to question the Lord's wisdom. He'd not only given me life, but eternal life, freely, through Jesus Christ. How dare I, a mere, puny woman who'd been given so much by grace, shake my fist in the face of the Almighty and demand an accounting for something I had not chosen?

As I looked upon the face of this helpless little one, I prayed, "Lord God, all children are gifts from You. I know You will give me what I lack. Help me to be the best mother to her that I can possibly be."

At that moment, maternal instinct took over, and I began to love my baby wholeheartedly. As a teenager I thought I'd never be able to care for a handicapped child, should I have one. The very idea left me repulsed. Now, in my early thirties, I knew better. *(After all, I still loved Debbie, who had become physically handicapped, didn't I?)*

Within a few minutes, Becky was taken back to the nursery, and I was wheeled away for further surgery.

When I awoke, Paul was with me in the recovery room. I struggled to consciousness to tell him, "Sweetheart, I'm almost certain Becky has Down syndrome."

A little grin curled upward from the corners of his mouth. His whole demeanor told me he didn't take my words seriously. What I desperately wanted to hear from my husband was that my fears were unfounded. Finally, to satisfy my persistent urging, he ambled down the long corridor to look at the baby through the nursery window. When he returned, he was pale. My fears were not a drug-induced dream.

He held me in his arms and prayed specifically for our tiny, fragile daughter.

"Lord, enable Becky to learn to read, so she can read the Bible for herself someday," he said. "We won't ask, *Why me?* but *Why not me?* We believe, Lord, that You are sovereign. You make no mistakes."

I wondered how many fathers would offer this as a first prayer for a less-than-perfect newborn. It confirmed what I'd known all along about Paul. Though short of stature, slender, and "bookish," he is a giant of a man in God's kingdom. We'd started our courtship while singing in a church choir. I had a large collection of music, and Paul teased me, "That's another good reason I married you."

Our home percolated with song those first six years of married life. We sang together as we played on the floor with our babies. We especially enjoyed singing when we were driving. School songs, campfire songs, hymns and choruses, patriotic songs, show tunes, children's songs -- we sang them all. My all-time favorite from my own childhood was "Somewhere Over the Rainbow." But stark reality draped around us like valley fog the day we brought our baby home. Her care likely would swallow an ocean of our time, energy, and resources. At this low point, the only music we heard in our souls was a dismal, ponderous dirge. A young family's sad song had begun. And, as far as I was concerned, there were no rainbows on the horizon.

Chapter 2
One Sweet Note

The day after Becky's birth, when I asked Dr. Veldstra point-blank if my baby had Down syndrome, his mouth formed an inaudible, "Oh." He quickly brushed the question aside by talking about something else. He didn't confirm the diagnosis until the day before we left the hospital.

"I'm curious. What made you ask me about Down syndrome so soon after she was born?" he said. "It usually takes a month or six weeks before parents ask what's wrong."

"I've seen babies like this before," I replied. "As a matter of fact, my youngest sister has it. She was the ninth child in the family, born when my mother was 42 years old."

"That's when most Down syndrome babies are born, at the end of the regular childbearing years," he said, sadness softening his words, "not at your age. I hadn't wanted to tell you quite yet, after all you'd been through."

In sharp contrast to the doctor's concern, songs of discouragement and insensitivity had already begun.

If you are a new parent, grandparent, or good friend of someone with a Down syndrome baby, I want to assure you that the following experiences probably won't occur today. We are now better informed, more sensitive to one another, more careful about making hurtful, judgmental remarks. Terminology has changed, too. I am recounting these only to show how far we have come in dealing with tender spots touching the core of our hearts.

My first encounter with insensitivity was while the baby and I were still in the hospital. A 23-year-old mother of newborn twins came next door to visit me when Becky was two days old.

"Hey, I just found out that somebody in this here hospital had a baby that's a *mongolian idiot*," the young woman said. "Boy, if it was mine, I'd put it right into one of them institutions. I just can't stand *retards,* ya know? I tell ya, I sure feel sorry for whoever them poor parents are."

Utterly shocked, I was speechless. She prattled on about her own life's trials. With the newborn twins, she now had five children. Her husband had left their home in her seventh month of pregnancy, after badly beating her with a two-by-four board. The babies had come early but were doing fine.

Suddenly I wasn't even insulted by her reference to Becky as a *mongolian idiot*. All I could think was, *And this woman feels sorry for us?* After all, we had a strong, committed marriage that had already weathered several dark storms. I wondered how it would be possible for this poor, young, ignorant woman to care for five little children by herself.

Still I was totally unprepared by others' reactions to Becky. Since my newspaper editor wanted to know when my baby arrived, I phoned her after I returned home and was ready to go back to work.

She gasped profanely, using the Lord's name, "Too bad the kid didn't die before she was born!"

My first assignment back on the job was a Planning Commission meeting at City Hall. The planning consultant, a pleasant man I'd known for two years, greeted me, "Oh, you've had your baby!" Then he added with genuine

28

concern, "I hope the baby is okay. We heard you were having complications."

Another reporter, possibly thinking she'd make it easier for me, quickly spoke up before I could reply, "Her baby has Down syndrome."

Uttering a swear word, the otherwise well-spoken man added, "I pray that it dies!"

Once again I was so stunned, words failed me. That was the second time in as many days I'd heard the same message from well-educated professionals: my baby should be dead! I realized that neither of these people knew the Lord, yet I resented it that both called upon God in this way. In reality, they were showing themselves to be every bit as insensitive as the ignorant young mother in the hospital. I'd assumed that intelligent professionals would keep their negative opinions to themselves.

Worse yet was the reaction of our pediatrician in Modesto. Becky continued to lose weight for a month after we brought her home. She spit up most of the little she ate, and she had a severe cold.

During one of our many visits to his office in Becky's early weeks of life, Dr. Thorne *(not his real name)* took one look at her and shook his head.

"Do you really *want* her treated medically? Many people with babies like this just let them go naturally, you know."

We could hardly believe our ears. Paul, not easily angered, retorted, "Of *course,* we want her treated medically! That's why we're here. Just what are you suggesting, anyway?"

The doctor did some fast backpedaling. "Oh, I didn't wish to imply that we *shouldn't* treat her. I was just stating what *some* parents want."

As we drove home, Paul stated what I too was thinking: "We don't need Dr. Thorne's services any longer. We know our family doctor will do very well."

In the 1960's, rudeness and unsolicited negative advice from friends and strangers apparently was supposed to be gratefully received by parents of such a child. At least, we ran into a few people who were more than willing to share golden gems of wisdom with us.

One day a young woman I barely recognized as someone I'd met sometime, somewhere, stopped me on the sidewalk outside the grocery store.

"I've never seen a Down syndrome before," she said, peering at the blanketed baby in my arms. "Is that typical of those kind of kids?"

"It's typical of *babies*!" I responded, marveling that she'd never seen a baby sucking its thumb before.

An elderly friend wrote to us, "How soon do you plan to institutionalize your child? I understand these children are very difficult to deal with. It would be best to do this before you become attached to her."

"*Attached* to her?" Did this woman think we'd picked up a stray kitten?

Now I'm fairly certain this dear lady did not intend to add to our hurt, but at the time I wrote back curtly, "Becky will be sent away to an institution when someone can drag her over my dead body."

"Oh, Lord," I pleaded in prayer, "is there nothing but a sad song for us these days? Can't You give me some encouragement once in awhile?"

He gave me a brief glimmer of hope in response to that prayer when Becky was a couple of months old. I was rocking her, once again letting a vaporizer do its work clearing her lung congestion. She was having an especially hard time breathing. Tears were silently running down my cheeks as I wondered how long she'd be able to hang onto life.

Debbie, Jonathan, and David were banging on the kitchen floor, rummaging in the wide cupboard drawer for pots and pans I allowed them to play with. Debbie, now barely four years old, suddenly ran to me.

"Please don't cry, Mama! Jesus says she'll be all right!" she said, wiping my tears with her little hands.

I hugged her with my free arm and kissed her innocent, upturned face as my tears continued flowing. She left and went back to play with her brothers.

"Thank you, Jesus," I breathed, for this one sweet song of comfort. And to think it came through one of my own little children!

Not long after that, I re-read Dale Evans Rogers' book, *Angel Unaware*. Impulsively, I sat down and poured out my anguish to this well-known actress/singer, whose own Down daughter, Robin, inspired the book. Somehow I knew she'd understand. I tucked a snapshot of the kids in the envelope and mailed it. In a few days I received a handwritten response:

> *Dear Rosalie,*
> *Thank you for your precious letter. The picture of your children is so sweet.*
> *God understands every bit of your heartache over your little ones, but they are safe in His care --*

and He cares for you, too and must have a great confidence in your spiritual stamina to allow these things. However, what an opportunity for you to be a Christian witness through it all -- Rebecca looks like Robin!

God bless, renew your strength daily & give you the Peace that only He can give --

> *Sincerely,*
> *Dale Rogers*

Her note of encouragement amidst the barrage of insensitivity helped immeasurably.

One person, Paul's dear father, denied Becky's condition as long as he lived. We now smile at this notation he wrote in his family Bible:

Rebecca Icenhower, born in Ripon, Calif. Feb. 16th, 1964 (Sunday 5:30 PM). Born with Down syndrome? Doubtful!

Most of the time I could deal with the reality of my child's developmental delays, though at other times I was in complete denial. I kept weekly notes of her progress and was elated whenever her accomplishments compared favorably with early development stages, even if they came at the very outside edge of the norms. In the margins of a booklet the pediatrician gave us, I'd write what she'd done at a particular time.

Our annual *Icenhower Gazette* newsletter, mailed at Christmas, 1964, sounded optimistic about 10-month-old Becky's development. Actually, it is brimming over with denial:

"She was thought to be a Down syndrome baby at birth, but her progress thus far has been perfectly normal. She is bright and alert and gives no evidence of retardation. Rosalie has a private theory that the Lord, knowing her love of 'Things Oriental,' gave her this baby with almond-shaped eyes as a special token of grace."

Just a few months later, reality began to sink in. I wrote on the pages of the pediatric booklet, *July, 1965 -- 17 months. Becky does not do anything physical shown on these pages.* Illustrated items on the next several pages normally accomplished by infants 15-18 months old, are marked in pencil, *21 months.*

The gap was beginning to widen. Sad songs with their monotonous, discouraging words droned wearily around us with increasing regularity and intensity for awhile.

But then, how could we know what *delightful* songs were ready to pop around the corner?

DON'T SING ANY SAD SONGS

Chapter 3
Fun and Games

Before she turned three years old, it was obvious to everyone, including me, that Becky's development lagged at least a year behind that of a normal child. But she was especially gifted in what I called "fun and games." Many of these are songs of delight in our memories of those early years that too often were tinged with sadness and grief.

She hated the playpen from the time she discovered at 16 months that she could creep, though she resembled a crab with her backward crawl! She'd throw all her toys out of reach and then yell, clearly protesting her imprisonment, hoping the clamor would obtain her release.

Whenever I'd place her in the playpen so I could do something else for just five minutes, she'd pull herself to a standing position. She'd balance by leaning her body against the wooden bars, extending her arms upward in a pitiful invitation to any passerby, whether child or adult, to lift her out of her "prison." Failing to get attention by this, she would reach out and playfully grab my skirt as I walked past. Flashing a dimpled grin, she was completely charming, and I couldn't resist the temptation to pick her up. I'm convinced she knew exactly how to pull heart-strings.

But her games extended far beyond conning her parents into lifting her from the playpen. She was an independent explorer from the beginning, always learning at her individual pace, finding her own time and fashion to accomplish her goals.

She first stood alone at 16 months, soon after she learned to creep, never accepting help in getting to her feet.

Two months had passed, and as far as we knew, she'd never taken her first step.

* * * * *

One day she'd fallen asleep on the living room floor, where she'd been playing with some toys. Her dad and I left her there, not wishing to disturb her. The two of us were quietly talking in the kitchen when we heard Becky's familiar little giggle. We peered around the corner to see our newly-awakened 18-month-old walking from one side of the room to the other, enjoying herself immensely.

As soon as she discovered we were watching her, she plopped down and began playing with her toys. She pretended she hadn't the faintest idea what we were talking about when we praised her. She even refused to let us hold her up to let her feet touch the floor. She had a certain way of making her legs act like wet noodles!

For nearly the next year, we often saw Becky walking around the house when she thought no one observed her. We suspected our friends mused, "What wishful thinking!" when we told them she could walk, since she never demonstrated it when anyone else was around.

Then one Sunday the house was full of company for after-church coffee. Becky suddenly lifted herself up from a sitting position and strolled all around the room, glorying in the praise she received. She never fell down during her grand revue, since she'd had many months' practice in private. She was then two years, four months old.

Apparently she decided that as long as she'd made her debut, she might as well learn to be a climber, too. From that time on we never knew where we'd find her in the morning when we got up. She could be perched, fast asleep, atop the dining room table, her hands cradling her chin, her little rump in the air. Other times she might be spread-eagled on our high, narrow snack bar. There were even times we found her sleeping on the drain board of the sink!

One day when I stepped out the back door to check on the children, I heard a wee voice calling, "Mama, Mama!" Becky was in the tree house in the grapefruit tree. She had climbed the ladder but couldn't get down by herself. Fortunately, I was able to climb up and get her, though fear of climbing generally keeps my two feet planted on Mother Earth.

Another day, when she was three-and-a-half, I heard her from atop the garage calling, "Help me, Mama!" Now *that* was too much for me! As I've already said, I'm not much good at maintaining equilibrium more than a couple of feet off the ground. It was a good thing that Paul was home from his summer school classes, so he could rescue her.

Early in the morning, her own special systemic alarm clock apparently triggered "time to get up." Every now and then we'd wake up, startled to find every light in the house was on -- at 2:00 A.M.! We'd find Becky at her play table, happily pouring water from a miniature teapot into thimble-sized cups for herself and her teddy bears. Somehow she managed to climb up on a stool, turn lights on, fill the teapot, and get down from the kitchen sink without falling or spilling *too* much water.

Then there were the Missing Person Escapades, as we dubbed them..

From the time she started walking, Becky had developed a habit of edging through the picket fence into the Schoonhovens' yard next door. She'd rap on their back door, and these gentle, elderly neighbors would invite her in. They taught her to say, "Cookie, please." They adored her and looked forward to her once-a-day visit. Generally they gave us a call to let us know she was with them. But if they forgot to phone us, it was easy enough for one of us to check with them.

Paul's father spent a month or two with us each winter, and we traveled to Ashland, Oregon, to see him in the summer.

A family friend had come to see us at Dad's home, when Becky was three years old. We were catching up with her family's life since we'd seen her last. Suddenly I had the feeling I should check on our children who were playing in the fenced backyard. The three older children were playing tag -- but where was Becky? They hadn't the faintest idea!

"Mom, she was here just a minute ago," Debbie said.

We searched through the house, thinking she had come in quietly, gone into a bathroom or one of the bedrooms. We looked in closets and under beds, behind sofas and chairs. She was nowhere to be found. I panicked at that point and ran to the street calling, "Becky! Becky!"

Just then I saw a patrol car cruising slowly through the intersection of Allison and Union, two houses away from Dad's. I ran to flag it down to report our missing child. A happy little ash-blonde girl was sitting in the front seat waving merrily at me! The officer said he'd seen her standing in the middle of Siskiyou Boulevard, an extremely busy thoroughfare two blocks down the sloping street.

I was so happy to see her, I cried, vowing I'd never let that little tyke out of my sight again.

That was easier said than done, for we soon discovered Becky could not only squeeze through the narrowest of gateposts, but also climb over any and all other obstacles.

A couple of days after the Ashland Incident, as we unpacked our bags from our trip, Becky was missing from our yard. Paul went to check with the neighbors on either side of us, but they hadn't seen her. Taking the three older kids, we split into two groups to search around the block. No Becky. We were puzzled. Just how far could a short-legged, pint-sized three-year-old go in the ten minutes since we'd arrived home?

Finally we agreed we'd better get assistance, and Paul and the kids were ready to cross Orange Avenue to ask neighbors if they had seen her.

"Honey, why don't you call the police to alert them?" Paul suggested.

Just then we saw a patrol car coming down our street. You've guessed it -- there was Becky laughing and waving at us! The policeman was a man we knew. He grinned and lifted Becky out of the back seat.

"I kinda thought you might be missing something," he said.

A steely-eyed woman, a stranger to us, climbed out of the front passenger seat. She berated me well for my negligence, shaking a bony finger under my nose. She laid out some instructions, in no uncertain terms, to (a) watch my child better and (b) teach that child that it is *not* appropriate to walk into a person's house and request, "Cookie, please."

She huffily assured me, " I most certainly *did not* give that child a cookie, since it would not be in her best interests."

She had flagged down the policeman as he drove past her house, to report there was an obviously neglected child who had barged into her kitchen.

As soon as the patrolman and the indignant woman drove off, six-year-old Jonathan sent us into gales of laughter with his assessment: "Just think! Becky's only three years old, and she already has a police record in two states!"

Truly, Becky's escapades with "fun and games" were delightful. They lightened the songs in our hearts that too long had sounded like somber laments.

Chapter 4
Medical Merry-Go-Round

I resigned from the newspaper when Becky was eight months old. Struggling to care for two healthy, active boys, along with two little girls needing frequent medical attention -- and none of the children older than four -- was nearly too much for me. My energy, and I'd always had an abundance of it, was rapidly depleting.

For several years after Becky's arrival, it seemed as though a merry-go-round calliope cranked out songs alternating between "Oh, No" and "Not Again." We often pictured ourselves going in a circular pattern through revolving doors in the many clinics, doctors' offices, and hospitals we visited on a regular basis. Many weeks we wondered if we spent more time in the car and in waiting rooms than we did at home. The merry-go-round's programmed pattern seemed to be that if one of the girls didn't need to see a doctor, the other did.

Debbie's painful encounter with Juvenile Rheumatoid Arthritis was a daily battle but not life threatening. Becky went from one upper-respiratory crisis to another, ranging from severe croup to viral infections to pneumonia. From the time she was born, Becky *(like many children with Down syndrome)* had to be guarded closely against the possibility of severe colds blossoming into pneumonia.

One bright spot was in the picture. Her body systems recuperated more quickly than doctors expected. In fact, several times when Becky was hospitalized with pneumonia, the chagrined nurses had to search for her when we came to visit.

41

She discovered a way to escape from under her oxygen tent, sliding feet first from the high pediatric bed. Nurses apparently never noticed the elfin, barefoot creature slipping past the desk while they were concentrating on charts and doctors' orders! Usually they located her seated on the cold, smooth marble floor in the playroom, her miniature hospital gown wide open down the back to her diaper.

We gasped when we heard one hatchet-faced charge nurse, having all the charisma and grace of a battlefield general, barking orders to our two-year-old to "Stay in that bed! I mean it! You're gonna be in big trouble, lady, if we find you runnin' around again!"

A much more compassionate young nurse whispered, "Don't worry, Mrs. Icenhower. Her bark is far worse than her bite. We'll watch out for Becky."

Of course, Becky wasn't enduring great pain or being maltreated while she was in the hospital. She was the happiest, blithe spirit no matter where she was. But often I found myself on my knees imploring God to miraculously change Becky's chromosomal makeup. I would have gladly exchanged anything in the world to free her from Down syndrome, even my own mental acuity. But that's not an option one human being can offer a contract for.

One day I shared this with Olive, the saintly wife of a well-known Bible teacher. She told me how she, too, had begged God to make a bargain with her. I'd offered my mind to Becky; she'd offered her health and life in exchange for her husband's cancer.

She told me she had prayed, "After all, Herb is much more valuable to Your work with young believers and

42

seekers on university campuses than I am as a fulltime homemaker."

"Then," she said, "the Holy Spirit clearly directed me to Exodus 4:11-12 where the Lord rebuked Moses for complaining that he, being 'slow of speech,' was unable to deliver God's message to Pharaoh."

She read to me from her Bible, "And the LORD said unto him, *Who hath made man's mouth? or who maketh the dumb, or deaf, or the seeing, or the blind? have not I, the LORD? Now therefore go, and I will be with thy mouth, and teach thee what thou shalt say.*" (KJV)

(I've quoted this passage from the King James Version, because this is the way I recall hearing her read it. The New International Version hadn't been published then.)

"That morning," my friend continued, "the Lord showed me that I was exalting myself, that I really was saying, *I am wiser and kinder than You are.* I was making myself sovereign. Only the Father has the right to make decisions regarding my life and my husband's health, whether it means extended years or early death."

After pondering her words awhile, I was able to accept this word of admonition that I needed as well. I could not give Becky additional intelligence. I could not bear Debbie's pain, not ever. I could not protect my little boys against the hurts of life. Nor could I give my lungs to my husband, now that his asthma was steadily growing worse.

Some weeks went by. Then one day as I thumbed through a book in my husband's library, looking for a particular quotation I needed for a Bible study, I came across the first question and answer of Lord's Day I of the Heidelberg Catechism and the scripture references that follow them:

Question: What is your only comfort in life and death?

Answer: That I with body and soul, both in life and death, am not my own, but belong unto my faithful Savior Jesus Christ, who with His precious blood has fully satisfied for all my sins, and delivered me from all the power of the devil, and so preserves me that without the will of my heavenly Father not a hair can fall from my head; yea, that all things must be subservient to my salvation, wherefore by His Holy Spirit He also assures me of eternal life, and makes me heartily willing and ready, henceforth, to live unto Him.

Written in 1563, the Catechism's stiffly formal language and sentence structure seemed more than a bit overwhelming when I first read it, four hundred years after its publication. But slowly, slowly, I began to learn I can leave my life and my loved ones in the hands of our Sovereign Lord.

Paul changed his teaching position in the fall of 1966, going from the Christian school back into a public school classroom. While we remained loyal advocates for Christian school education, we celebrated two of the immediate benefits coming our way as a result of the change. These were better insurance coverage and a larger income. The family's continuing medical problems had held us near, if not below, the poverty level.

Surrendering our circumstances to the Lord, I found there were at least three other grateful songs to sing:

1) Though Becky was developmentally delayed, she had a lithe, active body strong enough to fight off those frequent bouts of pneumonia; 2) she had no signs of heart

44

problems that plague many Down syndrome children; 3) her vocabulary increased much more rapidly than we'd been led to expect. By her third birthday in 1967, she had 58 single words or combinations forming 2-4 word sentences, including "wha's dat?," "goody, goody," "more snacks," "more Cheerios," "gonna pray," "thank you," "hi, boys," and an emphatic, "I don't want dat!"

My weary body and sagging spirits were lifted. Gratitude for God's tender mercies changed my merry-go-round's grinding clamor to psalms sparkling with praise. This is one of the poems I wrote for a denominational magazine at that time:

My Grace is Sufficient
(2 Corinthians 12:9)

When exhausted and tired,
Alone I agonize in pain;
Then His presence hovers near
And gives me grace to smile again.

When within my poor faint heart
Alone I struggle unknown fear,
Then the blessed whisper comes,
"Be still, my child, for I am here."

And then, time and time again,
My sorrows He will bear,
And give me songs in the night
With grace to sing them anywhere!

Chapter 5
School Days

In 1968 four longhaired British lads, the Beatles, were singing about Sergeant Pepper, Elvis Presley was worrying about someone stepping on his blue suede shoes, and hippie guitarists were mellowing out in the Haight-Ashbury district in San Francisco. Our family was singing "School Days."

That fall four-year-old Becky entered an early childhood development center in Stockton. David was in afternoon kindergarten in the public school two blocks away from home. Both Debbie and Jonathan were enrolled in Ripon Christian School, Jonathan in second grade, Debbie in third. Paul continued teaching junior high math in Manteca. And wonder of wonders, I began studying at the college now known as California State University-Stanislaus in Turlock!

Admittedly, I was a bit apprehensive about competing with a generation of young people just out of high school. I'd graduated from the Bible School at Northwestern College in Minneapolis 15 years before; I was now 38 years old. Would I be able to juggle all I'd been doing: caring for our home, the children, doing some typing for Paul, *and* still keep up with college classes?

"How did I ever get myself talked into this?" I asked myself half aloud as I sat down for the entrance exam. I knew, of course, that I *hadn't* really talked myself into it. It was the small, still voice of the Lord convincing me through two sources within a few days' time.

First, I had read an especially poignant article in *Christianity Today* about the plight of children with mild mental handicaps, including Down syndrome, whose parents left them at hospitals when they were born. Many of these unfortunate infants were placed in state facilities for the "mentally deficient." Others were relegated to facilities for the mentally ill, of all places! In either case, the children were virtually abandoned by their parents. Few of them had the opportunity to be nourished or stimulated intellectually or spiritually, to be taught a trade or to interact socially outside those institutional walls. Of course, they did not develop as well as similar children reared in loving homes. I read the article several times and wept.

The second prompt from the Lord was in the form of a pamphlet issued by the President's Committee on Mental Retardation. Its message was that most developmentally delayed persons could be taxpayers rather than tax-supported indigents *if* there were schools and teachers training them, enabling them to work. I wondered if I should become a teacher.

Frequently in our married life, we've found that God guides us by simultaneously bringing the same thing to our attention. This was one of those times. Paul also had been thinking perhaps I should go back to school, but for a different reason. His health was declining at an alarming pace. His asthmatic condition was sapping his energy, draining his life away.

"If the Lord should call me home to heaven, how would you be able to support yourself and the four kids?" he asked. "I think it's something we should be concerned about."

That was the understatement of the year. Our small town, population 2,000 at the time, certainly wouldn't

48

afford many opportunities for a well-paying job. We had no savings because of that gigantic backlog of medical bills still absorbing most of our resources like a giant sponge.

"I canceled my life insurance three or four years ago," he reminded me, "because we couldn't afford the monthly premiums and still pay the medical bills. Now that our finances are a little better and we could squeeze it into our budget, I can't get the policy reinstated because of my health."

Tuition for Californians was extremely inexpensive in 1968: the total cost for fees and books was less than seventy-five dollars a quarter. We figured our budget could handle that if we put a pittance away each month before school began the last week of September.

I opted for a full class load three days a week, so I could spend as much time at home as possible. Meal planning and cooking ahead erected no particular barrier, for that was what I had done for years. I did laundry early in the morning; cleaning could wait till I got home in the afternoon. The children were cared for before and after school by our friend Grace in her home across the street from Ripon Christian Elementary. Paul helped by washing the supper dishes and getting the kids ready for bed so I could study.

In the meantime, Becky's school in Stockton, 23 miles away, started its new term the day after Labor Day.

She enthusiastically clambered aboard a shiny, yellow bus at 7:00 A.M. and dragged her weary little body back into the house around 6:00 P.M. After such a long day, our tiny girl, less than three feet tall, weighing 28 pounds, often fell asleep on the bus. Once she nodded off

49

while eating dinner and woke up the moment her face hit her plate of spaghetti.

Nevertheless, Becky proved she was her own person in a miniature package, even at four years old. She demonstrated that on the very first day she came home from school. As she bounded down the school bus steps, she turned and waved to her schoolmates still aboard.

"G'bye, you goofy guys!" she called out with gusto, while we blushed with embarrassment. *(What if a stranger within earshot thought we had taught her to say that?)* Never had her enunciation been clearer.

It was obvious that Becky did not think of herself as "developmentally delayed." She was intelligent enough to recognize there was a vast difference between herself and some of the bigger, older students. Many were unable to walk or talk; some still wore diapers. Abilities and skills she was learning at home were reinforced at school. What was developing through this consistent training would mean for her future, we could not know then.

But for the time being, our family's favorite melody was "School Days, School Days." Had anyone asked, "What did you learn today?" each of us could have added a chorus or two of our own!

Chapter 6
Folk Songs and Legends

A few of Becky's escapades over the years have become absolutely legendary, worthy of a new round of Gilbert and Sullivan operettas. Sometimes they have been completely innocent or inadvertent. Other times her wonderful timing and sense of humor certainly have made our folk songs of life memorable.

Several of them have been in connection with church services.

Every couple of years, Becky loses her hair. I don't mean she sheds a *few* hairs on her collar or bed pillow. Like many other children and adults with Down syndrome, she literally loses every hair on her head for a month to a year at a time. Then, with or without medical treatment, just as mysteriously as her hair disappears, it begins to grow back, often with a slightly different shade and texture. How long it will stay intact, nobody knows.

People around town were used to Becky's hair loss and paid little attention to it. But in parks, playgrounds, or restaurants, concerned strangers sometimes wondered aloud if she were receiving chemotherapy for cancer.

Attempting to keep her looking as normal as possible when we were away from home, we'd bought a child-size wig for her when she was four years old and bald as a boulder.

We were on vacation and so were in a different church the first Sunday she wore the wig. The sanctuary was long and narrow. There was no air conditioning. Not the slightest hint of a breeze was stirring, though the narrow, arched stained glass windows were open. And it

51

was nearly too hot to breathe! All around us, women opened their purses and whipped out colorful paper fans. Men shed their blazers, loosened their neckties and collars. That didn't help much, so some of the fellows self-consciously folded their bulletins and wagged these improvised coolers under their perspiring chins.

Halfway through the service, Becky had had enough. That wig was just too uncomfortable! Without a second thought, she flipped it off her head. It sailed straight up toward the vaulted ceiling and fluttered on down again.

A startled lady in the row ahead of us squealed, "A bat!" Every neck craned to see. Little gasps of excitement rippled through the pews around us. I calmly reached up and plucked the fluttering dark brown wig out of the air and neatly tucked it in my purse.

Jonathan, sitting to my left, nearly had a conniption trying to stifle his giggles. None of us dared to look at one another for fear we'd burst out laughing. But we've always wondered what those startled parishioners thought when they saw me slip a "live bat" into my purse!

Perhaps because of her own experience with wigs, Becky had an uncanny ability to spot toupees as well.

Our pastor's brother, visiting from another part of the country, was a stranger to us. We hosted a weekly adult Sunday school class in our home across the street from the church, and the pastor brought his brother along that morning.

The usual pleasantries were exchanged, and everyone settled down with a cup of coffee and a cookie before the lesson began. In a brief moment of complete quietness, pint-sized Becky walked over to where the stranger was seated and patted him on the shoulder.

"And how are *you*, Mr. *Hair*?" she asked, emphasizing what none of the rest of us had spotted.

The poor man turned crimson with embarrassment while his brother, the pastor, nearly choked with laughter.

We were so familiar with some of Becky's spontaneous, innocent responses that we scarcely noticed what she was doing until some uninitiated stranger became indignant or embarrassed.

From the time she turned two until she was about eight years old, Becky clapped her hands and smiled broadly, or occasionally giggled, whenever she placed her money in the morning offering. One Sunday after services, a couple from out-of-town admonished me that this was "unseemly behavior," and "a child should be taught appropriate conduct in God's house."

Huffing with self-righteousness, they left before I could explain.

But Debbie understood something that those strangers apparently didn't. At home she told me, "The Bible says that the Lord loves a cheerful giver, right? So He sure must love Becky."

To us, her simple act of praise illustrated a combination of Mark 10:15, "Anyone who does not receive the kingdom of God like a little child will never enter it," and Proverbs 15:30, "A cheerful look brings joy to the heart."

Our family agrees that Becky's most infamous "church story" occurred when we were visiting dear friends living a stone's throw from the Mount Hermon Christian Conference grounds near Santa Cruz, California.

One evening we decided we'd go hear a well-known professor from Dallas Seminary. We arrived at the auditorium a bit late, and the usher located the only seating available where all six of us could sit together -- in the very front row.

The speaker preached his heart out, reaching the climax of his sermon with a rhetorical question, "Is there *anyone, anywhere* who can honestly say, *'I have never sinned'*?"

His biggest mistake was in making a slight dramatic pause. Five-year-old Becky seized the moment. She popped out of her chair, waving both arms, shouting, "I can! I can!"

A surprised hush fell over the audience, and then a tumultuous roar of laughter erupted. The good professor stepped back, mouth agape. He looked positively stunned for a second or two; then he began to laugh also until tears ran down his cheeks.

"Well," he said, wiping his eyes when things finally quieted down, "is there anybody *else*?"

Other incidents outside of church settings have cinched Becky's place as a living legend in our family. For instance, after she became completely potty trained at five years old, she could never pass a toilet without wanting to use it. Once I caught her, just in time, with her dress up and her panties down, ready to try out the bathroom display in the Sears store! I swooped down in a flash, and ran with my surprised, kicking, screaming child along the narrow corridor to the ladies' room. I'm not sure she ever did understand why I'd snatched her from the most convenient location she'd ever seen in the mall. *(I carefully avoided Sears for a long, long time after that.)*

Besides ruining the conclusion of a sermon and livening up the Sears display, Becky added to her repertoire by admonishing a customer in the grocery store.

An unusually obese woman just ahead of us at the checkstand was ready to pay for a jumbo-sized chocolate bar. Becky dashed up to her, patted her on the tummy, and admonished her, "You put that back! You don't need that. You too fat awready!"

Undoubtedly Becky was practicing what she once told my sister-in-law Gayle, "If I'm anything, I'm honest."

I hate to admit it now, but I didn't stick around to see if the customer put the chocolate bar back. I wheeled my grocery cart around and headed down the nearest aisle. Not for the world was I going to claim that kid as my own! I didn't even pause when I heard a little voice yelling after me, "Mama! Mama! Where you going?"

By the time she caught up with me, everyone knew she was mine anyway. I might as well have kept my place in the checkout line!

Years have passed, Becky has grown up, and she doesn't pull the same kind of shenanigans any more. Now she reminds us of our own foibles and foolishness when she figures things are getting way out of hand. We and our other grown children and our grandchildren can get pretty silly when we're together for special occasions. After standing aside and observing a certain amount of our foolishness for a time, Becky exhibits her intolerance by scowling and pursing her lips. Another minute more is just too much!

Becky plants her size 5 feet firmly in our midst, folds her arms, scrunches a frown on her brow and calls for reasonable decorum: "Can't you people just act *normal?*"

If Becky is anything, she's honest, you know!

Perhaps her innocent comedy is not in competition with Gilbert and Sullivan operettas, but it contributes some delightful notes to our folk song of family legends.

Chapter 7
Climb Every Mountain

The incredible panorama of the Pacific Northwest, with Mt. Rainier to the south and Mt. Baker to the north, often reminds me of the opening scene of "The Sound of Music" -- and the mountains of growth Becky gained the summer we moved from California to Washington State.

Had we not moved, Becky never would have found the opportunities she has now. But that's getting several years ahead of the story.

This is how it all came about.

Paul's breathing problems increased so greatly throughout the summer of 1972, we knew he'd not be able to return to his teaching position in September. Several times I didn't think I could get him to the emergency room at Manteca Hospital in time to save his life. One memorable afternoon we made the trip three times, each a race pushed by near-panic. The hospital personnel couldn't admit him without his physician's express instructions, and Dr. Veldstra was out of town. Finally an emergency room doctor came to the rescue with an injection.

Through the rainy, cool fall and winter months in Central California, from November through January, Paul found breathing much easier. Clear, crisp days, beginning in February, when smudge pots belched their thick, black blanket over the budding orchards to counteract frost hovering in the air, he gasped for oxygen. From past experience we knew with the dry heat coming later in the spring and summer, his distress would intensify again.

One evening in early spring, 1973, Paul expressed something I'd not known he'd been thinking about.

"Honey, let's pray about moving to the Seattle area, where it's wetter, cooler, and has clean air all year," he said. "I don't know if I can survive another year here."

Paul knew the Seattle area and its weather well. As a junior high student, he'd spent a summer with his aunt while studying cello at Cornish School. Years later, after his stint in the U. S. Army, he returned to Seattle to complete a degree at the University of Washington. The more we prayed about our future, the more convinced we were that we should move at the end of the school term in June.

The two of us flew to Seattle one Saturday where Mr. Palmer met us at the airport. He was the developer of Hollyhills, a new residential area of large mobile homes and lots sold as a "package." It was within the city limits of Bothell, north of Seattle.

"This is the four-bedroom house we like, and this is the lot we'll buy," we told the developer, "*if* we decide to move."

We returned home the same day, prayed for a week, and decided we'd move in July.

But our children didn't exactly dance the cha-cha when we told them, "Pack your things, kids. We're moving to a place called Bothell, Washington." Kids can't hear the music when they are being uprooted from the only home and friends they have known all their lives.

Debbie had completed her first year of junior high; Jonathan finished sixth grade, and David fourth. Becky left her San Joaquin County special education school in Manteca.

One of Paul's former colleagues at Ripon Christian, Allen Kosters, offered us a "deal we couldn't refuse," to drive a giant U-Haul truck loaded with his furniture and

58

ours. He had accepted a principalship in Washington. Sharing the cost of a do-it-yourself move was a great saving to both families, and much easier on Paul.

Once we arrived and settled into our new home, we scurried about getting the kids their new library cards, signing them up for recreation programs and jump-starting their music lessons, to help them find similarities with their former activities in Ripon. Next on the list was to complete their registration for school for September. We visited a half-dozen schools and academies before registering the three older children in the Christian school adjacent to the church we began attending. Becky would be enrolled in a public school special education program.

In the meantime, I made the transition from teaching high school English to "domestic management." Wild blackberries grew profusely in our area, so I canned quarts and quarts of them, besides baking cobblers, and pies. One day while I made jam, a process that required my full attention for a time, a not-so-minor miracle occurred.

Becky, entertaining herself while her siblings rode their bikes, brought a small book to show me.

"Wha's dis word, Mom?" she asked. I told her, only to have her return seconds later with another question: "But wha's dis word, Mom?"

"I don't know what kind of game she's playing," I whispered to Paul, "but she seems to be completely immersed in that book."

The next day she again interrupted my activity, pulling at my skirt to get attention. She was showing me the same book. This time she opened it to the first page and read it aloud, perfectly, word-for-word! I'd told her each of those words just once, twenty-four hours earlier, and she'd remembered each of them.

For some time we'd remarked about the "mystery" of her ability, from three years old on, to select a specific children's record by title from a stack of thirty or more. If she said, "I play 'Jack an' the Bean'talk' now," that's the one she'd place on her tiny record player. All the records were identical, as far as we could see; all the same size and color, black with yellow labels. Only the titles were different.

"There must a slight scratch mark on the label or some unique characteristic she picks up on," we reasoned. "But if that's true, how can she identify so many of them accurately?"

As teachers, we were familiar with the basic sight reading lists compiled by Dolch and other educational gurus.

"It has to be sight reading," Paul decided as she now read to him from the book in her hand. "Somehow she's managed to memorize the words by their placement and shape, maybe even recalling what words are there by the pictures on the page."

Yet she went on to read new pages in other books. Dr. Seuss books were suddenly thrilling adventures in reading, though some of his silly, concocted words were difficult for her.

By another week, she began snatching the newspaper as soon as it hit the porch, excitedly reading the headlines aloud as she bounded though the door to present it to me: "Here's you paper, ma'am!"

After dinner one evening, the other three children and we were taking turns reading a verse or two of a scripture passage for our devotions. Becky announced, "I take turn, too!"

From that time on, we enjoyed her "performance." Uninhibited as any ham actress, she read every selection as if it were Shakespearean drama. She especially liked the passage beginning in Luke 8:28, where Jesus healed the demon-possessed man living in the tombs: "When he saw Jesus, he cried out and fell at His feet, shouting at the top of his voice, *What do you want with me, Jesus, Son of the Most High God? I beg you, don't torture me!*" *(NIV)*

She threw herself to her knees, hands clasped in earnest supplication, her performance worthy of an Oscar.

Drama aside, we realized this was a very real answer to Paul's first prayer for her at birth, that someday she could read the Word of God for herself. Convincing school personnel that Becky should be placed in a reading class was quite another matter. The notice we received three weeks before school was to start, indicated Becky's placement was in a "training class," where students would learn to sort long items from short, green from red, identify stop signs, gender logos on bathrooms. She'd already done this for the past five years.

I made arrangements to meet the teacher, who looked at me with blank disbelief when I mentioned "reading."

"Mongoloids," she said, using the passe' word for Down syndrome, "do not read. She may be word-calling, but that's not *really* reading, you know. She probably doesn't understand one bit of it."

Unable to convince her otherwise, I made an appointment with the principal to plead Becky's cause.

The same old tired song I'd heard before fell from her lips: "You have to understand, Mrs. Icenhower, that these children do not read. Her records show she has a measured I.Q. of 36, you know."

I could nearly see neon lights blinking in her brain, *Here's another one of those mothers deep in denial!*

However, I persisted until she finally agreed to meet Becky and test her the next day. All the rigorous skepticism of my child's reading ability had been a prejudgment, since neither the teacher nor principal had met her yet.

After the brief assessment, the principal looked up in astonishment.

"My goodness!" she said. "Becky reads at a third grade level. How long did you say she's been reading?"

Throughout the summer Becky's learning curve was one of rapid acceleration in acquiring other skills as well. She swam like a dolphin, bobbing and arcing through the water as if it were her natural habitat, worrying our neighbors at the Hollyhills pool to no end.

"You just can't let her swim in the deep part," they'd caution me. "That little kid could drown, you know."

Of course, that might be a possibility. She was such a tiny girl that even in the shallow end, she could be in water over her head if she waded. Since I'm a non-swimmer, I'd have to depend upon others to rescue her, should it come to that. Her brothers and sister played and swam with her while the lifeguard and I watched, but we didn't tell her to stay out of the deep water. Admonitions died out in a few weeks as the critics saw she was never in trouble as she swam.

Toward the end of summer, she became fascinated with bicycles. She'd long ago outgrown her tricycle. We gave it away before we left Ripon. Now she begged for a bike of her own as she watched her siblings zip up and down the hills on theirs.

"I get a bike, okay, Dad?" she'd ask.

One day Paul stopped at a garage sale on his way home from the grocery store. There it was, a miniature black bike just right for Becky's short legs. He bought it, though he wondered the rest of the way home just why he had.

She'll probably never ride it, he said to himself.

Becky jumped up and down in wild excitement when she saw the two-wheeler. She immediately christened it "Black Beauty" and referred to it as her "hoss." For several weeks she made no attempt to ride it. She walked it around the yard and house, talking as if the vehicle understood every word.

When we called her in for lunch, she'd respond, "Wait till I tie my hoss up fust," while hitching its imaginary reins to an invisible post.

"Shall I show you how to ride your bike?" her father volunteered.

"No, Dad," she said firmly. "I don't want to."

In those first nine years of her life, we'd learned to accept that Becky had her own time schedule, her own agenda, and her own way of problem solving. Apparently that applied to learning how to ride a bike as well as everything else. One personality trait that is commonly associated with Down syndrome is a penchant for digging in the heels until she is good and ready to do something on her own. We left the topic of bike riding alone.

Several weeks went by. Then out of the blue she let us know this was the moment she chose to ride the bike.

"Come watch!" she called, her blue eyes sparkling with excitement.

Paul thought he should hold onto it while she made her first attempt. She pushed the bike part way up the hill, hopped on, and whizzed past him before he could get to her side!

During the next week or two she had a couple of minor spills, but soon mastered riding in virtually no time at all. The worst accident she had was when she turned her head to see what might be behind her -- and ran smack-dab into the rear of a parked car. Fortunately, she wasn't seriously hurt. She hobbled to me for comfort, dried her tears on the back of her hand, and immediately climbed back on the bike and rode off.

"Black Beauty" ceased to be a horse. It was now a *bicycle*, the joy of her life. She could ride it to her heart's content on our quiet street where few cars traveled.

Becky's favorite song that summer was from "The Sound of Music." It seemed to us she'd chosen an appropriate theme, "Climb Every Mountain." But from our view, Mt. Rainier and Mt. Baker were mere bumps on Earth's surface compared with her growth.

Chapter 8
Becky and the Bard

Becky's life blossomed like fireworks in a summer sky after she learned to read. All facets of language, from naming animals in categories to an amazing fascination with Shakespeare, erupted with a bang.

Her vocabulary expanded rapidly after she and I invented a word game one morning while we watched out the window for her school bus. She selected a category each day.

"Mom is a goat," she might start.

"Well, that's O.K. Becky is a sheep," I'd reply.

"Tha's O.K. Mom is a pig."

We branched off into naming farm animals one day, zoo animals another, fish or birds the next. She loved the humor of it to think of Mom as an ostrich or camel or elephant, and she amazed me with the many living creatures she could name in the proper categories after a few weeks. But I could break her up into hysterical giggles anytime by saying, "Becky is a duckbilled platypus."

Unfortunately, she also learned a few other "strange" words. When she first started attending the early childhood center in Stockton, California, she came home with a whole string of profanity that would stun a pirate. The amazing thing is that she placed the words in the "right" places in her sentence structure.

Becky learned that this was not acceptable language long before we left California. Since she didn't use it any more at home, we assumed she didn't use it at school after that, either. But soon after we moved to Washington, we learned she used it at Girl Scout meetings instead! This facet of our darling daughter's life was unknown to us until the no-nonsense leader called me one evening.

"I'm afraid we're going to have to ask Becky to drop out of our Girl Scout troop," she said, "unless she cleans up her language."

Truly puzzled, I questioned, "What do you mean?"

Then I wished I hadn't even asked.

"Parents should be more careful in using those kind of words in the home," the woman admonished. "After all, children repeat what they hear, you know."

By the chilly reception on the other end of the conversation, I could tell the lady didn't buy my story that our family never used that kind of language, at home or elsewhere.

"Shame on you, Becky!" I scolded her, looking and sounding as fierce as possible. "You can't even go to Scout meetings any more if you say naughty words."

"I be a good girl," she promised, her bottom lip quivering. "I not say bad things no more."

She would do nearly anything in the world to remain in her special Scout Troop. That harsh warning from her leader -- and a sterner lecture from her father than I gave -- pretty well cured her.

She found an alternative word on her own that she apparently thought was every bit as "scandalous" but wouldn't get her in trouble. When she wanted to be daring or a "little bit wicked," as Debbie called it, Becky would sidle up to friend or stranger and impishly say in a stage whisper, "Underwear!"

When this word didn't provoke the shock value she wanted, she gave it up.

Then, somewhere along the line, Becky fell in love with The Bard. As an English teacher, I owned a set of ten Shakespearean plays on long-playing stereo records. She astonished us the first time she came home from school and politely asked me, "May I listen to Shakespeare, please?" *(Is there any other adolescent anywhere in the English-speaking world who asks to hear Shakespeare records?)*

"Hamlet" soon became her favorite play, and she became its dictatorial director after dinner.

"Okay," she'd say in her bossy little way, "I be Hamlet."

Then, pointing to us in turn, she assigned our roles.

"Debbie, you be Ophelia. Jon, you be Claudius; David, you be Larry." *(She meant Laertes, of course.)* "Dad, you be Polonius, and Mom be the queen."

She'd begin with a passionate mumbo-jumbo sounding as if it could be one of the brooding Dane's soliloquies. Then she'd pause and point to one of the rest of us. The chosen actor would try to come up with something she'd accept as authentic, but she was a tough taskmaster. Our command performances were just that: commands!

"Now that not right at all!" she'd scold. "Now *listen* this time!"

She'd repeat her previous speech, slower and much louder, as the unfortunate character attempted to pick up on his cues. We'd manage to finish the scene, after a fashion. Without a doubt, Will Shakespeare is still spinning in his grave.

Thousands of Shakespeare fans throng to Ashland, Oregon, each summer for the city's Elizabethan theaters. Soon after Becky discovered The Bard, we made one of our trips to Ashland, not to see the plays, but to visit relatives and friends. We were window shopping when Becky spied a T-shirt with Shakespeare's picture on it.

"Oh, Mom, Mom!" she exclaimed. "Could I have that, please?"

"Of course," I said, seeing stars sparkle in her pretty eyes.

"Would you like a name on the back of it?" the young salesclerk asked. "You can have the color of your choice for the lettering."

Becky didn't give a hoot about the color of the letters. And any name would be fine, as long as the letters were H-A-M-L-E-T!

When she was 17, Becky learned American Sign Language at school. The communication disorders specialist worked with Becky and other students with their pronunciation and enunciation skills. Becky's tongue was often "lazy," making some words unintelligible to others. Two deaf students in the class were learning basic sign language. Becky quickly picked up the fundamentals, astonishing the specialist.

"I've never seen anyone learning ASL so quickly," she told me.

Becky begged us to buy her the textbook, so we did. Since she could read, she was able to look up the signs she didn't know. She became so proficient with ASL that sometimes she was asked to help interpret for deaf students in other classes.

Since then, she's able to minister to hearing people as well, especially with her graceful signing of "Silent Night" at Christmas. It's become almost a tradition for someone to ask her to "perform" it while the audience sings. With poise and confidence, she has signed for as many as 300 people in an audience. Now every three years or so, she takes a refresher course in signing.

Now I do not wish to lead anyone astray. Becky is *not* a savant in the area of language. Her accomplishments simply illustrate that a person with mental impairments, even with a measured I.Q. of 36, is *sometimes* capable of learning and enjoying appropriate aspects of language as other people do. Her level of understanding, of course, is lower than that of a person with average intelligence. Certainly, not all Down kids are able to communicate effectively. As with any segment of people, capabilities vary widely. Some are much more capable than Becky; others cannot even say "Mama."

Whether or not a Down child or adult speaks clearly enough to be understood by others, it is reassuring to know: "Before a word is on my tongue, you know it completely, O LORD!" *(Psalm 139:4)*. God understands all we say or intend to say, no matter what our label or ability. He only asks us to join together and "sing, all of you who are upright in heart" *(Psalm 32:11)*. The Holy Spirit carries our prayers, smelling like sweet incense, before the Father *(Psalm 141:2)*. No intelligence test has to be taken, for salvation is by grace alone, through faith alone, by Christ alone.

The Bard's richest sonnets pale and fall away when compared with a simple prayer uttered in faith. Becky, like the rest of us, would learn that.

DON'T SING ANY SAD SONGS

Chapter 9
Wedding Song

In April, 1980, a young man named Jim Putnam came to ask Paul for our Debbie's hand in marriage. They had met on the University of Washington campus, where both were students. We had known Jim for a few months and knew he was a fine Christian fellow. We were pleased to give them our blessing.

"Mom, I'd like to have Becky as one of my bridesmaids," 20-year-old Debbie said as we made plans.

Surprised, I said, "Oh, Debbie, are you *sure*?" I thought she might be thinking we expected her to ask.

Looking me straight in the eye, she confirmed this as her own choice, "Of course, Mom. She's my *sister*."

Debbie has given us many proud moments in her life. She is a wonderfully gifted musician and writer. But we've never been prouder of her than at that particular moment.

Betty Stryker, wife of the principal at Everett Christian School, where I was teaching at the time, sewed Becky's formal gown.

Becky, all. a-dither when it was delivered, pranced around from one room to the next, preening and posing before every mirror in the house. Practicing the measured steps as she hummed her off-key version of the "Wedding March" became her first ritual every morning and the last each night.

Proclaiming to everyone within earshot, "I goin' to be a bri'esmaid!," she fairly floated through the rehearsal. "You know how I *love* weddings!" she exulted over and over.

During the ceremony, though we were sitting in the front row of the church, Paul and I nearly missed the exchange of vows. Our eyes were not glued on the bride, but on Becky. We were afraid she was going to faint. We realized she was in trouble when the rose bouquet she carried started shaking. Nearly imperceptibly at first, her body began to sway from side to side, first one way; then the other. Finally she was lurching forward and back, her face growing paler and paler. One of the other bridal attendants reached out and softly touched her arm. That seemed to calm her down.

After the ceremony, I asked, "Are you okay, Becky?"

"Oh, Mom, I jus' so *scared*!" she answered. "I dizzy. My head goin' awound!"

Being in her sister's wedding is one highlight of life Becky will never forget. Neither will some of her teachers. You see, there were times, over the next couple of years, when she wore her bridesmaid's dress to school without our knowledge!

When we ate together at breakfast, Becky would be wearing her regular school clothes. My school day began much earlier than hers, so I left the house an hour or more before she did. Apparently she'd get the urge to deck herself out in the off-shoulder, ruffled, full-length formal after I left. She'd manage to dash out to the school bus without her dad seeing her. Then she'd change when she got home in the afternoon, before I arrived.

We'd never have known about this "switcheroo," except she'd dutifully hand me a note from school that usually said something like this: "Please try to teach Becky to dress appropriately for school. A bridesmaid's gown causes problems at school."

School personnel also had "problems" when she swapped her school garb for a sun suit or summer shorts in the dead of winter on a few occasions. I imagine her former teachers are still saying, many years later, "Remember that crazy family that let their daughter wear such outlandish outfits to school?"

"Do you 'member, Mom," she reminisces, "how I be in *two* weddings? I be a bri'esmaid for Debbie and Jim, and I did the guest book at my bruvver David and Angie's wedding."

Thankfully, she doesn't wear any of her wedding garb any more, probably because it "mysteriously" disappeared from her closet several years ago.

In July, 1992, Becky's oldest brother, Jonathan, flew with his fiancee, Marlene Ernst, to the British Virgin Islands to be married aboard a tall ship and sailed away on their honeymoon cruise. Of course, Becky didn't participate in that wedding, but she often gazes at the pictures and talks about it anyway as if she had.

"'Member when Jon got married?" she asks. "I do. It was on a sailboat."

As a young teen, Becky declared she was going to marry Luke Skywalker, her "Star Wars" hero.

"Good luck, Beck!" her brothers told her. "He's not real. He's make-believe."

After they finally convinced her he was a fictional character, she shrugged her shoulders and said, "Oh, well, I marry Donnie Osmond instead!"

Indignation turned to scorn when she learned from a television newscast that Donnie had married.

"That does it!" she exclaimed. "I 'fru' with him!"

Now in her thirties, one of her favorite pastimes yet is tracing bridal gowns from a specialty catalog.

Finally, several years ago, she told us solemnly, "I decide I stay single all my life." She made this decision after she dated a developmentally delayed *(non-Down syndrome)* fellow a few times. He told Paul on a number of occasions that he wanted to marry Becky some day.

"I drop' him, though," she confided to us. "He was a two-timer."

"What do you mean by 'two-timer'?" I asked her, not sure she knew the meaning of the term.

Her explanation showed she understood. The young man was also seeing another woman with Down syndrome at the same time he was professing his undying love for Becky.

Paul reminded her, "You know, Becky, it's better to find that out now rather than later."

"I know," she replied. "I need *(to be able)* to trust him."

She went out for dinner *(a bacon-burger, fries, and Coke)* and a movie with a developmentally delayed young man this past spring, chauffeured by a fellow on the staff of Cascade Christian Home.

"But that was *not* a date," she informed us. "He jus' my friend."

A young man with Down syndrome, who lives in our city, has identified himself to us and his coworkers as "Becky's boyfriend." Every time she is home to visit us, she insists on visiting him at a nearby grocery store, where he works as a bagger. They have known each other since they were children in school.

"We don't date," Becky informs me, as though that's news to me. "He's my friend, too, not my *boyfriend*. No wedding song for us!"

DON'T SING ANY SAD SONGS

Chapter 10
A New Song

Becky, like all adolescents, went through her teen years with erratic highs and lows, crankiness and jubilance, stubbornness and cooperation; a quirky, unpredictable medley of laud and lamentation.

Our family always has Bible reading and devotions at the table twice daily, after breakfast and after dinner. She loved the Bible stories from early childhood and looked forward to going to church every Sunday.

However, when she became a teenager, her behavior changed. This certainly was not a new concept for me to observe, since I am a specialist in adolescent growth and development. She displayed the know-it-all attitude many other teenagers have. If she didn't like something we said or did, she'd stomp to her room and slam the door, staying there nearly half a day, pouting.

When she turned eighteen, Becky began taking greater interest in the Word when we read it aloud or when she read it to us. Her attitudes toward others began improving, too. Now, if she was perturbed with us, she still fled to her room and slammed the door, but she popped out again in twenty seconds or less, saying, "I sow-y, Mom 'n' Dad. Jesus doesn't like me act like that, does he? I sow-y!"

The church where we were members has a strong family orientation and Biblical theology. One practice we particularly appreciated as the children grew up was the annual visit by the elders.

The congregation is divided into districts with elders held responsible for the spiritual growth and development of members in their designated areas. Once a year two elders visit the homes in their districts, specifically to give help and encouragement. The family is expected to read an assigned portion of God's Word several times before the visit, so they can discuss it when the elders arrive.

In January, 1983, the evening the two men for our district were due at our home, Becky came to me, asking, "You tell elders I want t' make p'ofession of faith? I love Jesus; I want t' follow Him."

"No, Becky," I answered. "You'll have to tell them yourself. Jesus wants *you* to confess Him as your Savior. That's one thing your mom can't do for you."

She said no more about it and, quite truthfully, I forgot all about it as I prepared dinner and took care of grading a batch of papers for my class.

When the two gentlemen arrived, Paul welcomed them into the living room. There was the usual small talk for a few minutes.

One of the men, politely acknowledging Becky's presence, asked, "And how are you, Becky?"

Quickly she answered, "I love Jesus. I wanna suhve Him all the days of my life. I wanna make p'ofession of faith." She spoke every word clearly as possible, an earnest expression on her face.

The startled elder looked at me, mouth agape.

"Is this *her* idea?" he asked. "Or is it something you told her to do?"

"It's her own," I replied. "She asked me earlier to tell you for her, but I told her it was something I couldn't do for her."

The elders arranged for the next step a few weeks later. She was to meet with the board *(the Consistory)*, to give testimony of her faith in Christ. This would allow the leadership to discern, as far as humanly possible, that Becky knew what salvation in Christ means and how it translates into one's everyday life.

Understandably, she was nervous about meeting the Consistory that Sunday morning before church. It is a solemn and somewhat intimidating thing for any teenager to do.

"You come wiv me, Mom?" she asked, pulling on my hand as we approached the Council Room.

An elder intercepted me at the door.

"I'm sorry, but you'll have to wait here," he said. "Parents can't come in with their son or daughter. We want to be sure young people are expressing their own convictions."

Becky looked devastated.

"*Mom!* " she begged, grasping my hand tighter. "Please come wiv me! Tell him, Mom!"

"Well, all right," the elder said, apparently satisfied he had at least obeyed church regulations by giving me the information.

Those already in the room gave us a warm, friendly reception as we entered. Pastor Peter Holwerda smiled at Becky and indicated a chair next to him.

"Come right over here, Becky, and sit by me," he said.
I found a chair next to her.

Several elders asked simple questions about her faith, and she answered with clear assurance. The last one to speak asked a wordy, convoluted question, at least fifty words long. I wondered how anyone could have followed its wandering "rabbit trail" and be expected to know what it had to do with anything! Frankly, I was glad *I* wasn't the one who had to answer it.

Becky didn't hesitate for a moment. Taking the pastor's hand and looking up into his face, she pleaded, "Pete, jus' tell him I love Jesus, and all I wanna do is suhve Him, will you?"

Chuckles ran like electricity around the room, and several elders nodded their assent.

"You know, Becky," Pastor Holwerda said, "that's good enough for me, because I'm sure it's good enough for Jesus."

In this denomination, the elders indicate their approval for those desiring to make public profession of faith during the morning service. Usually, candidates making profession stand and face the platform as their names are called. They answer the pastor's questions, and at the conclusion, give a brief word of personal testimony. Then they come forward for the "right hand of fellowship." Or sometimes a large group may choose to walk single-file to the platform as their names are called, respond to the questions, then give their individual testimonies.

Becky surprised the congregation -- and her parents -- by hurrying straight to the platform the moment her name was given, quickly answering the pastor's questions. Then, poised and confident, she turned toward the several hundred people in attendance and expressed her same sweet, simple testimony.

"I jus' love Jesus so much, and I wanna suhve Him all the days of my life," she said.

There wasn't a dry eye in the sanctuary that morning. Some of us could hardly sing the closing hymn. But angels were singing joyful praises before our Father in Heaven.

Chapter 11
Song of the Open Road

A recurring song of sadness tugs at the heart of anyone responsible for a special needs child who cannot fully care for herself. What will become of this "forever-child" in future years?

Sometimes family caregivers deny the need for planning. Is it because most of us don't like coming to grips with our own mortality? Regardless of my own initial reluctance at first, Paul and I took steps in early married life to meet our responsibilities toward one another -- and our obligations of parenthood -- by planning for our family's future needs, particularly for the possibility of our early deaths.

We had our wills drawn up soon after Jonathan was born, when Debbie was slightly over a year old. Codicils for David and Becky were added later. While they were all minors, we designated our pastor *(with his agreement)* as the one who would see to it that the children were placed in a Christian home.

As Becky grew up, we asked each other some other important questions.

"What if, for instance, we should be killed in a car accident, then what would happen to her? Who would take care of her? Where would she live?" Paul wondered. "Suppose someone would be willing to take the three older kids, but not Becky?"

"Yes, we'd better think this over," I replied. "Even if both of us survive to a ripe, old age, then find ourselves unable to care for our own needs, how could Becky fend for herself?"

When the children became adults, we rewrote the wills, with Debbie named as guardian of Becky's care. Still, we hoped it would not be necessary for any of our children to make a "have-to" place in their homes for her. What we really wanted was some type of arrangement made for a suitable, permanent home in the very probable likelihood we'd precede her in death.

While we still lived in Ripon, we made an initial contact with Salem Christian Home, a large, well-respected residential facility in Southern California. Now that we were in Washington State, placement in California was too far away from all the rest of our family. Several Lutheran facilities in our area have excellent reputations, but *(as with all such places)* there are few openings for new residents. None, of course, can hold a reservation for a possible need in the nebulous future.

I completed my Master of Education degree in special education at the University of Washington and worked as an administrator for a vocational training school for mentally challenged adults for a couple of years. I was well aware of rapid expansion of non-church related group homes in our particular area. But not even one among the many facilities met standards for my professional recommendation to parents or guardians. They were often dirty, smelly, and poorly administered. Few were fiscally well-run; some were dingy, bleak shelters that seemed to meet barest living essentials. Staff, in a few cases, were barely more competent than the clients. How, then, could we even think of one of these places for Becky?

Then, in 1979, a representative of Salem Christian Home spoke to an interested group of people in our church after a morning service. He outlined plans for a new residence, Cascade Christian Home, being constructed near Lynden, Washington, about 100 miles north of our home in Bothell. Primarily, it would house twelve developmentally delayed adults *(six men, six women)* who were able to care for their own personal needs.

Residents also were to have the mental and physical capacity and dexterity to learn work skills outside the four walls. Building of the ranch-style home was being funded through several local churches, organizations, and numerous individuals.

After the meeting, Becky climbed into the back seat of our car and said, with her usual bright confidence, "Cascade is my *real* home. I live there someday."

We were astonished that she had come to this conclusion on her own, for we hadn't said a word about it during the meeting or on our way to the car. She was about 13 and, like all teenagers, optimistically thinking ahead about leaving home.

Her internal music box had automatically switched the tape from "Home, Sweet Home" to "Song of the Open Road." For at least the past year there were little indications this was coming, but we'd unconsciously ignored many of them.

Her special education classes and the things we were teaching along the way were strengthening her wings to fly away from us. Encouragement from classroom and home, combined with other learning experiences, and self-determination were pulling her toward independence.

From the time Becky was nine, we insisted that she make her own bed. I helped her change the sheets each week, but she was to make it up daily before leaving for school, just as the other children did.

Her cheerful announcement, "Come, see it, Mom," came when she thought the bed was ready for inspection.

At first it was hard for me to look at the lumpy, bumpy mess of blankets, sheets, and spread. When she occasionally fussed and whined about "all that work" she had to do, I didn't allow her to give up. Eventually her skills improved, and the grumbling stopped.

Despite her reluctance the first time or two we asked for her help, she gradually became less dependent upon the rest of the family in other ways as well. She was *always* a step ahead of her siblings in taking care of her clothing. Her sister and brothers were typical teenagers who didn't mind clutter. Becky put *her* clothes on hangers! Her dresser drawers were Martha Stewart-perfect, because she carefully refolded *everything* in them every day! *(I wish I could say she learned that from me.)*

Several days a week she flitted around the house, dusting furniture, and with great ceremonial pomp and flourishes, she set the table for dinner.

These, of course, were some of the independent living skills she needed for the future.

Both Debbie and David liked to bake, and they often asked Becky to "help" them. She learned a few homemaking skills at school, such as preparing her own snack, breakfast or lunch, though little cooking was involved. At home, Paul sometimes let her stir the soup as it was heating, a task she liked, but we never allowed her to open a can of soup or to make her own sandwich.

"It's obvious to us now, isn't it, Paul?" I asked at that time. "It's our fears, not hers, that keep her from learning to do simple cooking on her own."

84

As she matured, she stayed at Fort Lewis, Washington, for weekend Special Olympics events. The first time, she looked as sad as a basset puppy when we left her with others in the assigned barracks. I dared not turn back to look at her small, pathetic face. I knew if she showed any sign of tears, I couldn't leave her there.

Of course, we went to watch her in her swimming, running and jumping events and celebrated her gold and silver medals.

At the conclusion of the first weekend, we picked her up from the barracks. As she climbed into the back seat to go home with us, she exhaled the deepest sigh I've ever heard: "Lucky relief!"

She never knew I'd cried all the way home when we'd left her and that my inward sigh upon her retrieval was every bit as great as hers.

But this was one very small, tentative step in my learning to let go of her, as dramatic for me as the astronaut's first walk on the moon. I wondered, in a poem I wrote for a Christian magazine, how soon and how far she'd fly on her own:

DON'T SING ANY SAD SONGS

God Remembers the Sparrow

When you go, Little Bird, tell me:
How far will you fly?
Will you merely skim the ground
Or mount to heav'n on high?
Will you fly from your nest afar
Or stay near, content?
Will you burst the vaulted blue --
Will you make the attempt?

Will you sing among the clouds
And notes to angels lend,
Or hum among the buttercups,
Sunshine and daisies blend?
Does anyone but God know the
Song you'll sing, Dear Bird?
Will your song thrill the universe --
Will it even be heard?

Fly! Fly your highest, your best;
May your song be heard!
And fear not tomorrow's storm --
You're God's own Little Bird!

Chapter 12
Becky's New Home, Sweet Home

In late January, 1983, Paul received a phone message with good news/bad news. Good news: Becky was on a short list of three applicants being considered for an unexpected opening at Cascade Christian Home, nearly four years after she applied. The bad news: the vacancy came because a young woman from the home had stepped off a city bus, walked into the path of a car and was killed instantly.

"Let's not tell Becky about the possibility of her moving just yet," Paul wisely counseled. "She was so upset the last two times she thought she was going to Cascade."

First, she'd been a potential resident on a list of five others who had applied; the second time she was on a list of four. In the latter case, two clients moved from Cascade into an apartment of their own. The young women replacing them were being released from a State facility for the handicapped and had nowhere else to go. Their families did not want them.

The current situation was distressing to me. I knew Becky wanted to go; I knew this was appropriate. But I still wasn't ready to release her.

And to think a place in the home was available because a developmentally delayed Cascade resident named Joyce had died in a traffic accident! My own emotional state made me feel guilty about that young woman's death, though I'd never met her.

On Tuesday afternoon, February 1, Paul shared more news when I came home from school.

"Cascade called," he said, "and they'd like Becky to move in as soon as possible."

Becky all but jumped out of her skin when we told her. She giggled and twirled, jumped and shouted.

"Yahoo! Tha's like goin' 'way to collitch *(college)*, isn't it, Mom? Like Debbie and Jon! Like my bruvver David go to Air Force!" she said, prancing around the room. "I go live at Cascade!"

A whole list of things needed to be done before we could make the transition on Thursday: sorting and packing her clothes, trophies, and "precious things;" notifying the school district about transferring records; telling the district's transportation department that she'd no longer need the school bus; calling the Social Security office for assistance in transferring Becky's benefits to the Bellingham office; getting a substitute teacher for my own class of fifth graders.

First of all, I called Becky's beloved teacher, Pat Pierce, to let her know what was going on.

"We'll take her to Lynden on Thursday," I said, "so Wednesday will be her last day."

"Oh, please send her to school on Thursday as usual," Pat pleaded. "Give us time to arrange a farewell party for her. She's been with us for such a long time. She'll want to say goodbye to all the kids and teachers, and we need to properly tell her goodbye, too."

The other calls I made that day sealed the reality of the matter for me. For the next twenty-four hours, I began exploring the territory of Bunyan's "Slough of Despond." It is one thing to write a poem about letting a birdling fly; it's quite another to experience it.

88

Becky went off to Sorenson School in high spirits on her last day. Paul helped me pack up her clothes and her precious belongings. Feeling absolutely numb, I asked myself, "Can this really be happening?"

At 2:00 we went to Sorenson to pick Becky up. The friendly secretary sent someone to bring Becky from the athletic field where her class was having P.E. It was five or ten minutes before a tiny person came in, weeping, head bowed.

"Oh, Mom!" she cried out, throwing her arms around me.

"Honey, what's the matter?" I asked.

The principal and secretary attempted to talk to her and tell her goodbye, but she sobbed and shook her head.

"I need Mom!" she said, laying her head against my chest, her shoulders wracked by her sobs.

Finally, Paul took her hand and led her to the car.

"What's the matter, sweetheart?" I asked again, as I buckled her into her seat-belt. "Were you hit by a ball or something?"

"No," she said. "Things jus' too sad today."

She couldn't utter another word at that point.

With a start, we realized it had suddenly dawned on our daughter that she was leaving home and this school *permanently*. She had been at Sorenson from its opening. She was mourning her loss of all that was familiar, her home and church, her family, her school and peers, all on the same day.

I silently chided myself, *Why hadn't we expected this? Have I forgotten the emotions I felt when I left my parents' home, after I graduated from high school?*

We drove north on Interstate 405 and switched to Interstate 5 in a few miles, mostly in silence. Becky had stopped sobbing but was still sniffling. I handed her a tissue but couldn't turn around to look at her. My own eyes were brimming with tears, and I was afraid I'd break down completely.

As I've said before, it's been our family's habit to sing whenever we travel -- old campfire songs, patriotic songs, school songs from elementary school days. Mostly we sing hymns. Even now, Paul started singing.

Immediately I felt a gentle tap on my left shoulder.

"Mom?" a tiny, quavering voice asked.

"What is it, Becky?"

"Wha'ever you do, don't sing any sad songs today, will you? Things jus' too bad today," she said, sorrow hanging in her throat like autumn fog over a meadow.

"No, Becky, we won't sing any sad songs," I assured her, knowing full well that I couldn't possibly sing any song at that particular moment, sad or otherwise.

Five or ten minutes later her weeping subsided to muffled sobs; she was making a grand attempt to stop altogether. I feared it would trigger a new wave if I broke down while singing. Perhaps thirty minutes after that, when I'd partially regained my own composure, Paul and I began to sing together, being careful not to sing any "sad" songs.

"Maybe," I said under my breath, "this will cheer her up, and she'll realize this move to Cascade is exactly what she's wanted to do for a long time."

After a bit, she went to sleep, her head resting on the window, as she often does. She even snored a bit. *She*

90

probably didn't sleep well last night, I thought. *I didn't either.*

She stirred awake as we approached Lake Samish, a clear, azure lake nestled in the mountains. I watched her in the rear view mirror as she gazed out at the sun-sparkled water. Then I felt another soft tap on my shoulder.

"Hey, Mom! What would you do if you saw the Loch Ness Monster *right now*?" she said excitedly, sounding like her usual self again.

Hamming it up dramatically, I replied, "Oh, Becky, I'd be so *scared*! I wouldn't know *what* to do!"

"Ha! Not to worry, Mom!" she laughed. "You'd have to go to *Scotland* first!"

Her sunny countenance didn't last long, however. She slumped back against the seat, quiet and somber, pensive. How different she was today -- not the effervescent daughter we'd cherished for nineteen years!

We turned off the freeway into Bellingham onto the Guide Meridian toward Lynden. Paul and I had seen Cascade Christian Home only once before, when we'd stopped to look it over on our way home from a trip to British Columbia a couple of years earlier. Now Paul asked me to watch for our turn-off at King Tut Road.

"King Tut Road!" Becky exploded in a gale of laughter.

"Yes, honey," Paul said, "Cascade is on King Tut Road."

Five years before, we'd taken her to see the magnificent King Tut Exhibit when it was in Seattle. She'd been fascinated with the boy-king of Egypt ever since.

"Now I live on King Tut Road!" she said, giggling.

Good! I thought. *She's over her apprehension or depression, whichever it was.*

I was wrong. As we pulled into the drive at Cascade Christian Home, Paul said, "Well, Becky, here we are. Here's your new home."

"No," she said firmly. "I not going. I stay wiv you."

"Becky," I reasoned, "this is Cascade, where you said you wanted to live."

"I not getting out of dis car," she said with strong determination.

"Well, then, why don't we just get out and stretch our legs and take a quick look?" Paul said gently. "Then if you don't like it, you don't have to stay."

Knowing she had an option, she bounded out of the car and quickly walked to the entrance ahead of us. Mark Mouw, the administrator, opened the door just as she reached for the bell.

"Hi!" he greeted her with a wide smile. "You must be Becky. We've been waiting for you!"

That's all it took to trigger Becky's usual happy, optimistic nature.

"Hi, ever'body! I'm here!" she called, immediately going in search of other residents who were watching TV in the family room.

Within a few minutes, while we were getting acquainted with Mark, she came back with Judy in tow.

"Mom, I got a bes' friend awready!" she announced, a smile wreathing her tear-stained face.

By the time we were ready to head back home, she was deeply engrossed in conversation with all her newfound "best friends."

92

"We have a welcome party for you tonight," one of the young women said.

Our daughter is excited about a party any time, especially if she is the center of attention. The nicely decorated room she would share with Dorothy thrilled her, too.

"See, Dad? I got my own closet, my own desk, my own dresser!" she exclaimed.

I whispered to Paul, "She has her own room, her own closet, her own desk and dresser at home. Maybe she didn't expect anything more than a bare cell here!"

She could scarcely tear herself from all the "magnificence" of her new home to tell us goodbye.

For me, the long drive home was painful beyond description. Every mile registering on the odometer wrenched me farther away from my "forever-child." We had been asked not to see her for a month, for the sake of her adjustment to the new arrangement away from us. Waves of incredible sadness, like giant ocean billows, engulfed my soul.

What have we done? I rebuked myself over and over.

Our home now seemed like a desolate wasteland. Every room, once bustling with non-stop activities of four teenagers, stayed neat. Areas formerly vibrating with their music, laughter, homework woes, and squabbles, were silent. Paul and I were alone, "chickless and childless," for the first time in nearly 23 years. I'd not realized the empty nest syndrome would grab me.

I was fine all day with my lively class of fifth graders, a truly delightful group. I loved teaching and planning all kinds of creative activities with them. But during the long, quiet evening hours, whether I was grading papers or reading a book, a sense of loneliness nearly overwhelmed me.

Paul's personality is far different from mine, fortunately, or we'd both have been residents of Pity City. He is pretty much of a loner during the day, buried in the companionship of his books. He missed the children, certainly, but he continued to concentrate on the Bible studies he was writing and leading. I focused in-depth on the children's absence, especially Becky's.

During the next month I went though all the classic stages of grief -- denial, anger, bargaining, depression, and finally acceptance.

In the denial stage, I sometimes awoke in the night, almost sure I heard Becky calling for me. Walking past her bedroom door any time of day, I had the impulse to go in to talk with her. Without thinking, I continued to set the table for three instead of just the two of us.

Anger, in the second stage, was neither well defined nor rational. I was alternately angry with myself for allowing Becky to leave us, angry with Paul for not insisting she stay with us, angry with God for taking her away from me.

I bargained with God to just let me have her back home. I'd plead with Him to let her live with us the rest of our lives.

The one consistent element of my grief was depression. I cried every night of that long first month she was away. Guilt lay heavily on my heart. It was though I had taken a third- or fourth-grade child to a strange place and dumped her off on a lonely roadside to fend for herself.

The loss I suffered was much the same as one feels in grieving the death of a loved one. Yet I felt guilty about *that*, too; my child had not died. It was more that she was *misplaced*, and I was the one completely to blame for that.

Of course, it was completely irrational. But as a result of my experience, I am not so quick to judge others as "spiritually challenged" when they "sing their sad songs"! Through this experience, I learned more of our gracious Father's compassion. He is the one who understands our human weaknesses and forgives our sins of complaining. He is the one who brings "psalms and hymns and spiritual songs" to dispel dirges of sorrow and grief.

Even so, the healing balm of God's love takes time.

Practically the first thing out of Becky's mouth when we saw her in March was, "I missed you so much, Mom and Dad! I cry ever' night in bed."

Still clinging to my fragile repertoire of sad songs, I held her close and said, "I did, too, Babe. I did, too."

DON'T SING ANY SAD SONGS

Chapter 13
Trust and Obey

Becky's graduation from Redwood School in Bellingham is one event we'll not forget! Becky and her classmates were garbed in red caps and gowns, each young woman carrying a single white rose. They entered the auditorium attempting to step to the cadence of "Pomp and Circumstance." Proud parents and pleased friends stood to their feet and clapped.

Here all similarity to a plain, ordinary high school graduation stopped.

Paul and I stifled our giggles behind our programs when we saw our daughter trying to shape up everyone around her. She walked with dignity, carefully adhering to the measured steps, head held high. But she seemed absolutely focused on reminding the fellow ahead of her to act appropriately, as if she were a drill sergeant.

"Straighten up! Walk right! Watch where you going!" she commanded in such a loud stage whisper everyone in the small auditorium heard.

The fellow behind her was just as "bad," as far as she was concerned. She reminded him several times, "Quit that! Don't act so goofy!" Once seated on the stage, which took some fifteen or twenty minutes to maneuver, the same young man began barking and howling like a dog.

"You jus' be quiet now! Sh-h-h!" Becky admonished him, to the great amusement of the entire audience.

But the howling and barking resumed each time the guest speaker paused. The distinguished gentleman didn't linger over his thoughts after the first few yelps!

That summer after graduation Becky worked in a sheltered workshop in Bellingham, filling a contract for fish hooks used in commercial fishing. We were amazed when we visited the job site a couple of times and saw how quickly and efficiently she assembled the parts on the moving conveyor belt.

The following year she had instruction in commercial dishwashing and fully expected to find work in a hotel or restaurant kitchen. She became quite discouraged and depressed when a job didn't materialize. She applied for cleaning and kitchen work in nursing homes and hospitals as well. One job was tentatively offered, then withdrawn.

"Mom, why won't they give me a job? I work hard. I do good," she said.

"I don't know, honey. We just have to wait sometimes," I replied, "until God says 'yes, now this is your time.'"

Meanwhile, dedicated counselors at Cascade taught Becky numerous new skills. They continued to cover many new topics, including safety issues. Encouraging each resident, according to ability level, they supervised and reinforced previously learned tasks, as well as taking on new challenges. For instance, with their guidance, Becky became adept in using the telephone to make appointments or to call for information she needed, and took her turn with other residents in helping with kitchen work.

For awhile Becky was paid to do laundry for everyone living in the home, but some kind of governmental regulation prevented her from continuing to do that.

After she'd been at Cascade for three years, the staff urged Becky to travel on the Greyhound Bus from Bellingham to Everett, where we would meet her, to spend the weekend at home. Up to this time we'd continued to drive the long trip to Lynden to bring her home and back when she had free time.

"But I don't wanna come onda bus. You come get me, please?" she begged her father over the phone.

Several program directors at Cascade kept insisting that she must learn independent travel, taking her through the process over and over. And Becky just as stubbornly resisted putting their lessons to use. Finally, she realized there was no other way she could come to see us except getting aboard that dreaded public transportation.

To tell the truth, the whole experience made me a bit nervous, too. Ten years before, when I supervised a vocational school for handicapped adults, I urged parents to allow their sons and daughters to become as independent as possible. But, again, when it came to my own daughter, I wasn't quite so sure it was good for her.

What if she inadvertently got off at the wrong stop? Would she know what to do if she did? Suppose some shady character persuaded her to get off with him somewhere along the line? I relaxed, but only a bit, when I learned the bus had only one stopping point between Bellingham and Everett. Another resident, already a "pro" in bus travel, was getting off at that stop in Mount Vernon.

Everything went smoothly on the maiden voyage. Nevertheless, she got off the bus looking distressed and weary.

"I don't like da bus," she said, looking at her father. "You take me home on Sunday? Please, Dad?"

She does need to learn independence, I thought, *and I can't hop in to rescue her from these experiences just because she's not comfortable the first time she tries them.*

And again I was reminded how many times I'd said the same thing to other parents! It would take me awhile to fully understand this was a first step in breaking the co-dependency chain I'd unwittingly forged between us for twenty-two years.

Her second bus trip didn't go nearly as smoothly as the first. Jonathan was home on vacation and offered to pick her up for us. He was a bit late getting to the depot, and the bus had already headed out for Seattle by the time he pulled into a parking spot. But there was no Becky waiting!

He called to ask if we knew for sure that she'd left Bellingham. After calling Cascade and confirming she had boarded the right bus, we phoned the bus station in Mount Vernon. No, she was not there, either. About then we received a telephone call from the Seattle depot. Becky was there, crying for her dad.

She had fallen asleep on the way and didn't wake up until she got past Everett. All passengers leave the bus when it arrives in Seattle, the major transfer point. When Becky got off and saw the huge station and hundreds of people milling about, she had no idea where she was nor why we weren't there to meet her. It was at this point one of the managers called us.

By the time Paul reached the station, a policeman had calmed her. She was enjoying a double-dip ice cream cone he had given her. I was the lady having the coronary at home.

Perhaps the most difficult thing I've ever done was to insist that she would take the bus home and back from that time on, no matter how much she begged us to drive her.

"My fears and misapprehensions cannot be allowed to cripple her opportunities for growth," I told myself.

Since then, she has purchased her own round-trip ticket in Bellingham and boarded the proper bus to Everett. Never again has she failed to get off at the right stop.

For many years she refused to check her bag through to her destination, apparently thinking she'd never see it again. She'd carry it aboard and cram it overhead or under the seat.

"No, I take it wif me," she'd say whenever anyone mentioned how convenient it is to check a bag.

In just the last two years she's accepted the procedure, surrendering her bags without a blink of an eye, to the care and keeping of the Greyhound company! We've noticed she has no difficulty reclaiming them at her destination.

Her first paid employment away from Cascade was a cleaning job in an office complex. She was consistent in thoroughness and attention to details. The job wasn't high-paying, but it was good experience for her to gain. Unfortunately, she had to take a taxicab because custodians began their work late in the evening, and the fare ate up nearly $400 a month.

Somehow, she managed to save up $75 for Christmas shopping. She brought the money with her when she came home for Thanksgiving and begged me, "Take me to the mall, Mom, please?"

It was worth the trip to see how well she made choices with the money she had. When we walked into the first store, she spied a display of Christmas mugs. She immediately selected one with Santa's likeness on it.

"This," she said with a grin, "is for Dad, 'cause he's our Santa."

She went on to find nice sweaters for her brothers, a fitted travel kit for her brother-in-law, and a box of twelve jars of jelly for her sister. She neither asked my advice or approval.

While she paid for her selections, I was nearby browsing a special sales table heaped with handbags.

When she joined me I said, "You made some great choices for presents, honey! Good job!"

She nodded. "Yep, jus' you left. What you want for Christmas, Mom?"

"Well," I answered, "I could use a new black purse."

"No," she said. "You got too many purses awready."

With that settled, she walked to another counter and bought me a pair of pantyhose instead!

Okay! I chuckled to myself. *She's becoming an independent thinker.*

"Becky's a little tightwad," one of her counselors at Cascade once told me. "She hates to let go of her money."

We prefer to think it's not so much that she's a tightwad as it is that she has more desirable goals for spending. Soon after she went to Cascade, she started saving until she had enough money to buy herself a marvelous stereo sound system. Sometime later she bought a television and VCR. She operates all these like a pro. *(Any day now, I suspect she will find that CD players are better than stereo records and make another change.)*

One year during my spring break, Paul and I planned to fly to Hawaii to see our son David, his wife Angela, and their children, Christopher and Andrew. Becky calls the boys her "matthews," her pronunciation of "nephews," and loves them dearly. When she learned of our plans, she managed her money well enough to pay her own airfare to come along. Though that was her first experience on a plane, she had no visible fear or distress.

A year later, she and two other women residents at Cascade flew to Disneyland with a Cascade chaperone for three days. They stayed in the Disneyland Hotel, toured Knott's Berry Farm and Universal Studios, and had a more-than-good time. Each young woman paid her own share of the expenses.

When she came home, Becky could hardly wait to tell me something of vital importance: "Hey, Mom! Guess who I saw at Disneyland?"

"We know so many people in California," I said. "And people come from all over the world to Disneyland. I can't possibly guess. Who was it?"

"*Mickey Mouse*, Mom!" she said excitedly. "An' I went up an' shook his hand an' ask him if he still remember' me fum when I was there b'fore. You know, when I was eight years ol'?"

"Oh, Becky, what did he say?"

Has she discovered that Mickey is a victim of long-term memory loss? I wondered. *Is she terribly disappointed?*

Instead, she looked at me as if she didn't quite believe me. Couldn't I grasp a far more basic fact?

"Mom," she said in a patronizing voice, "he doesn't talk, y'know. But he nodded 'yes.' Just think, Mom, he *still* 'members me fum then!"

"Believe me, honey," I assured her, "no one who's met you could *ever* forget you."

In the last several years she has taken several giant leaps forward in her semi-independence. The fact remains that she will always need a measure of supervision, but the need lessens as she gains new skills and confidence.

First of all, she moved into a duplex next door, owned by Cascade, and lived by herself for several months. Then another female resident moved in with her, paying half the rent and utilities. They cooperated in general household tasks; the apartment was kept tidy and fairly attractive, though mostly by Becky's initiative. They scurried about in the role of gracious hostesses whenever we visited, offering fresh-brewed coffee as soon as we arrived.

But the arrangement was not as compatible as it could have been. Her roommate was much larger, loud and bossy, and she hit Becky a couple of times.

Finally the young women, with guidance from the Cascade counselors, chose other arrangements, and Fran Armintrout has been Becky's roommate for several years. Fran also has Down syndrome and looks as if she could be Becky's sister!

In 1994 they moved into a comfortable, two-bedroom apartment in the small city of Lynden. With a combination of resources, using their own money and their parents' assistance, they purchased their attractive furniture. This past summer Becky bought a beautiful new recliner, a better computer, bigger monitor, and a computer desk.

Computer equipment? Yes, it's true! Becky pays her own bills by check and uses her computer to keep her checkbook and savings account balanced, using the Microsoft "Quicken" program. *(We all know some "normals" who don't do nearly as well with either computers or bank records.)*

104

She has her own outstanding "advocate," Becky Van Hofwegen, a Cascade Supported Living employee, who informs her of options and choices, keeps her accountable for keeping physically fit. She goes with Becky when she sees a doctor or dentist, helps her make decisions about clothing or larger furnishings. She also makes sure Becky's financial records are straight.

Becky and Fran do their own separate menu planning, cooking, and grocery shopping. Currently, they are taking weekly turns cooking dinner for each other.

For several years, Greta Einfeld, one of our friends in Lynden, went to the apartment once a week to study "Friendship" Bible curriculum with Becky. This series of lessons, specifically planned for developmentally delayed teenagers and adults, is designed for one-on-one study. Greta also asked Becky to read aloud to her. As a result, Becky's reading level, pronunciation, and comprehension increased substantially. We will be grateful forever for Greta's loving patience.

Our daughter has changed jobs several times after that first one in the large office building. The late night janitorial work she did for about four years gave her the needed experience to get a job with better hours. She found a better position as assistant janitor for a church congregation in Bellingham. She could go to work and back by city bus, a great saving from having to use a taxicab.

She loved her work and was commended for her thoroughness by getting an occasional raise. Unfortunately, several years later, the church suffered a split in the congregation, and Becky's job was eliminated when the factions went their separate ways.

Next, Becky worked with a crew cleaning offices at the Federal Building in Bellingham. Though the pay was good, her actual financial benefits were few. Again she had to take a taxi to work, this time very early in the morning. Once more, cab fare amounted to about three-quarters of her income, leaving little for anything else.

More recently she began working with a crew cleaning three of the international border stations between the United States and Canada, at Lynden, Blaine, and Sumas, Washington. The crew travels by van to the work sites, so transportation costs are reasonable. The only downside to this is that Becky has to get up at 4:00 AM; the best part is that she's home by noon.

It is a somewhat frightening experience for many intelligent young adults making the transition from home, moving out on their own. Sometimes it's even more difficult to change jobs. To know that Becky, still a "little girl" in many ways, handled these with aplomb is a great comfort to us. That she takes adult responsibility for her work, money, home and church, is a pure gift from Heaven.

"God helps me," she says. "I trust Him."

I, too, find that God helps me, and can instruct others how they, too, may depend upon the "Keeper and King" to care for their children.

When I have opportunity to speak to a group of young mothers, I tell them, "We moms can trust Him, the Sovereign King. It's *not* true that *Since God couldn't be everywhere at once, He made mothers,* as one popular saying goes. Mothers are completely incapable of being the lone protector, the shield and provider for their children. Regardless of the son's or daughter's needs -- mentally, physically, spiritually -- no parent can meet them all. Each day, often more than once, I commend Becky to the Lord's care and keeping, asking that a great legion of angels might surround her every minute."

"I jus' so lucky," Becky often says. "I got *two* homes and *two* churches," referring to her own residence and church in Lynden and ours in Bothell.

Several times we've been asked by Cascade Supported Living staff to meet with Becky, her advocate, and others interested in seeing her individual development expand. A week or two beforehand she is required to write a list of goals she wants to meet in the next year. At the meeting she gives a copy to each person invited to take part, generally those who keep her accountable in various settings. Then she is asked what she must do to meet these goals. We come away, amazed and full of wonder, seeing how well she presents her goals and how she thinks they can be accomplished.

Are things consistently wonderful for Becky? Has her I.Q. zoomed up toward the 100 mark? Of course not. She has trials as all of us do, some in the realm of misunderstandings or inability to express herself clearly. Is she a perfect person, an angel in disguise? Again, absolutely not! She has her failures, especially with lapses in truth. One of her current goals is to tell the whole truth, nothing but the truth, even when it is painful.

Several times, in the presence of her advocate, she wrote a check for "five dollars cash" for spending money and subtracted it from her checkbook. But at the bank, she put a "1" in front of the "5" and got fifteen dollars from the teller. This was all right in itself, since it is her own money, but she neglected to change her checkbook.

Of course, her records and the bank's did not match, and she insisted, "The bank make a mistake."

When her advocate showed her the returned checks, however, she acknowledged with tears that she had lied. She has other inconsistencies in her Christian walk, the same as the rest of us, and learns hard lessons just as we do. We're just a bit more sophisticated about it.

But God never lets any of His disciples off the hook of obedience just because they swallow Satan's line that people with a lower I.Q., or those in other unfortunate circumstances, are exempt. He expects all of us to sing "Trust and Obey" -- no exceptions -- "for there's no other way."

Chapter 14
Singing Along Emmaus Road

Br-ring! Br-ring! The green telephone on our night stand startles me. I turn over in bed, my mind a-jumble and disoriented. Attempting to focus my sleep-bleary eyes on the alarm clock, I mutter, "Six o'clock? Is it six o'clock? Must be a wrong number."

I close my eyes and struggle with temptation to lift the receiver and leave it off the hook. But after the fourth ring, I know exactly who is on the other end of the line. "Good morning, Becky!" I say.

"Hey, Mom! How you know it's me?"

"Lucky guess, huh?" I laugh.

"Today is Hallowe'en. My fav'rite holiday. You know. I dress up," she says. "Me and Fran and other peoples go to spin dance tonight. I read my story."

"What story?" I ask.

"I write a story 'bout Hetless *(Headless)* Horseman."

"You wrote a story?"

"Yes, on my compooter. It's *good,*" she says. "I read it at the party at Cascade."

"That's wonderful, Becky."

"I really call t' tell you 'happy birfday!' " she giggles. "I send you a card. You get it in the mail?"

"Yes, thank you, honey. It came in the mail yesterday."

"You like it?"

"Oh, yes, Becky, I like it. It's very pretty."

"I pick it out m'self," she says, then breaks into what loosely could be defined as a song. "Happy birfday to you, happy birfday to you!"

"Good job! When are you coming home for the weekend, Becky?"

"I come for Than'sgiving. Okay?"

"That's about four weeks from now," I remind her. "Tell Becky 'V.H.' to make the arrangements. Everybody will be here."

"My bruvver Jon?"

"Yes, and your brother David, all the kids and grandkids. You know, the usual gang," I reply.

"Gang? Gang? They not 'gang.' They nice," she giggles.

"Now you're being a silly-willy, Becky," her Dad butts in from the kitchen phone.

"Hey, Dad! You up?"

"Of course not!" he jokes. "Yes, I'm up. I'm making breakfast for Mom. When are you coming home?"

"I awready tell Mom, silly. I come day b'fore Than'sgiving. I tell Becky V.H."

"Tell Bill Gates he can come, too," Paul jokes. "He can bring pumpkin pie."

She draws the answer out with a slight trace of a whine. "Dad, I ca-a-a-n't! He got his own fam'ly."

The "Bill Gates routine" is something we joke about every now and then. It all goes back to when Becky and Fran moved into their apartment. Furniture stores were delivering new items. Fran's mother, Laverna Armintrout, Paul and I were carting our daughters' beds, dressers, chairs, clothes, plus all sorts of smaller things up the outside stairs.

"Say, young ladies, are you going to help us move or not?" Paul joked.

110

"Funny, Dad!" Becky said, picking up a Special Olympic trophy in each hand and carrying them. "This is it! You an' Mom carry the rest," she giggled.

Fran came trailing behind cradling a beautifully framed photograph to her chest.

"I bring Mary's picture. Poor Mary!" she said. "She died. I miss her so much. She's always good to me."

I casually glanced at the picture when she set it on top of Becky's TV. The woman's face was familiar because it had been shown on television and in full color in the daily paper. Mary Gates was a well-known philanthropist and tireless worker in social issues. She had died just a day or two before Fran and Becky moved.

Fran cut that out of the paper, no doubt, I thought. *She probably liked the attractive colors and pleasant face.*

After we returned home, I looked at the newspaper again. A smaller version of Mary Gates' picture accompanied her obituary. Her husband, William Gates; daughter, Libby Gates Armintrout; and son, William Gates III, were listed among her survivors.

Yes, indeed. I realized that Fran's brother Doug is married to Bill Gates' sister. Apparently Mary Gates *had* been kind and considerate to Fran. In all probability, she herself had presented that picture to Fran.

So Fran and Bill are aunt and uncle to the same kids! I mused. *That should teach me not to be such a skeptic! Why can't I take Fran's word at face value, until or unless she proves herself unreliable?*

I confessed to the Lord that I'd been much like those I'd inwardly condemned, those who doubted Becky's ability to read, write, and support herself.

The kindness of the Gates-Armintrout family is sincere and generous. Last summer Becky thought it would be fun to plan a birthday party for Fran. Her plans, of course, were simple ones: a picnic in a park, maybe go bowling afterward.

However, when Fran's relatives were invited, everything changed!

That's when Becky 'V.H.', Laura *(Fran's advocate)*, and Laura's husband loaded the van with Becky, Fran, and five of their friends from Cascade. They took a ferry from Edmonds to the Gates-Armintrout summer home. There they went exploring the area beyond the beach in an "awesome" motorboat with a driver provided for the occasion. Becky was the only one of her peer group to go inner-tubing behind the boat. The guests enjoyed a hot-dog roast, played volleyball, croquet, horseshoes, and many other games, then ate again.

At day's end, Fran's brother's gift arrived at the dock. It was a float plane chartered to fly the guests home to Bellingham. All but Becky 'V.H.', that is, who told me, "I didn't get to go on the float plane; I had the pleasure of driving the dumb van home alone!"

Our Becky, in the understatement of the year, told me, "Mom, they got a *beautiful* house! Bill Gates is *kinda* rich, I think."

Hats off to the generosity of the Gates and Armintrout families! And bigger hats off to Becky and her cohorts who have not one smidgen of awe-stricken, self-consciousness in their presence.

Dale Evans Rogers said her Down syndrome daughter was an "angel unaware." Another woman I've never met, the mother of a nine-year-old Down syndrome daughter,

112

wrote to me when Becky was a year old, "Kids like these have 'Emmaus eyes.'" More recently Lo-Ann and David Trembly wrote a book called *Emmaus Eyes: Worship with the Mentally Challenged. (See Chapter 18 for a review of this book.)*

The biblical reference is to two disciples walking along a dusty road to Emmaus after Jesus' death. They did not recognize the Risen Savior as He walked and talked with them. Later, as He broke bread and gave it to them, they recognized Him.

Family and advocates who know and work with children and adults with Down syndrome, generally say that those like Becky and her friends neither compare nor contrast their differences with those possessing superior wealth, fame and intellect. They have "Emmaus eyes" to see others, no matter who they are, as their equals.

They are also free to simply see Jesus as their Friend who walks and sings glad songs with them. We who consider ourselves "normal" are the ones who tremble, fumble for words and stumble over our feet in the presence of the powerful.

And, no, Bill Gates didn't come to Thanksgiving dinner at our house, bringing a pumpkin pie! You think our invitation may have been lost in the mail?

DON'T SING ANY SAD SONGS

Chapter 15
No More Sad Songs

Another occasion, another early morning.

The ringing sound -- somewhere between melodic and miserable -- continues, with a slight pause between, so it must be the phone, not the alarm clock urging me to get up.

Still in that slow-breaking dawn of consciousness, I groggily edge over to the side of the bed to look at the clock.

"Hello, Becky! I don't need a psychic to tell me who's calling," I manage to mumble.

"I no psychic. G'morning, Mom! How're you?" a cheery voice responds. "Happy Vowentine's Day!"

"Oh, Becky! Thank you for calling to say that," I respond, her charm immediately pulling me out of my fog. "And the same to you, honey. And, oh, thank you for the beautiful valentine we got in the mail yesterday."

"You welcome!" she says.

By this time, Paul picks up the kitchen phone.

"This is Darth Vader," he intones in the father-daughter routine they have perfected over the years.

"'Tis not, Dad. It's *you*!" she giggles. "You can't fool me!"

He asks, "How come you're up this early? Are you ready to leave for work, or did you get fired?"

"Oh, Dad! This my day off! *You* know!"

"What are you going to do today?" I ask.

"Stuff."

"Stuff? Like what? Run a race, catch a lizard, hug a tree?" I tease.

"*You* know, Mom," she responds. "Like I always do. Go to bank. Buy groceries. Exercise. Make vowentines for my roommate, Fran. We eat at McDonald's tonight. Maybe."

"Am I invited?" Paul asks.

"Oh, Dad! No! This is for *girls*. Mom, tell him it's just for girls!"

"Okay, Dad," I laugh. "You're not invited!"

She changes the subject: "Mom, Dad, remember my birfday in two days. Don't forget! Febwuary 16, you know."

"Yes, we remember. We were there, you know, when you were born," I remind her.

"And Dr. Veldstra?"

"Yes, honey. Dr. Veldstra was there, too," I assure her. "But changing the subject, Becky, when are you coming home for the weekend again?"

"Next Friday. Meet me in Everett, okay?"

"Same time as usual?"

"I think so. Ask Becky 'V.H' when. She's my advocate, you know."

"Yes, I know," I respond as I have dozens of times before. "Becky's advocate is Becky 'V.H.'"

Our daughter giggles. "You got it. Names the same. Becky 'I' and Becky 'V.H.'"

"Well, bring plenty of money with you so you can take me out to eat!" Paul teases.

"D-a-a-d!" she draws out the name with mock exasperation. "I bring money to go to McDonald's. Just *me*. *My* money. You buy your own!"

"Well, okay, if you say so," he concedes.

"Okay. 'Bye. I love you!" she says as she hangs up.

I lie back against my pillow, my mind and heart once again filled with awe at the amazing things the Lord has done for Becky in the sixteen years she's lived away from our home, the stretching opportunities she would not have had otherwise.

Throughout the year, she takes several community recreation/education excursions or classes studying wildlife, such as bats, sea life, or eagles; cooking, weight management, refresher classes in sign language, and others that strike her fancy.

Only one instructor has shown prejudice against her.

Becky signed up for a beginning tennis class, invested in a tennis racquet and balls, and merrily went to the first session. She'd watched Olympic matches on television, and was eager to learn. Her advocate agreed that tennis would be wonderful exercise. The two of them could practice together.

However, the young instructor refused to allow her to participate, mentioning in front of the others that Becky's "retardation" would be a distraction slowing the progress of the others. A few of the "normals" chuckled.

Becky was both embarrassed and devastated. Her advocate battled for and got the fee refunded. She also complained about the discrimination. Needless to say, that particular instructor no longer works for the recreation department.

On several occasions Becky traveled with her peers and a couple of advocates to Vancouver, Washington, to celebrate a Christian music festival called "Jesus Northwest." She also attends a similar summer weekend concert at "The Gorge at George," a natural amphitheater in the Columbia River Valley near George, Washington.

(Yes, indeed, there really is a town named George, Washington. The "founding fathers" must have had a sense of humor.)

After the "Gorge" event in 1998, Becky, Fran, and another Cascade client chose to sponsor a child through Compassion, International. The three of them split the $24.00 a month support for that little girl, and exchange pictures and letters with her.

Becky has accompanied us on trips to Honolulu, Atlanta, and to various sites in Oregon and California. But far more frequently she takes "package-deal" vacations with a specialized travel group to Disneyland, Universal Studios, San Francisco, and other fascinating spots she selects from a brochure.

Now and then she reminds us, "I been lotsa places you haven't been."

But several years ago, the return trip from a vacation was a nightmare for us as well as for her. She went with a recognized special travel agency promising us, and Cascade, that they would see Becky from her doorstep and back. Cascade clients had used this service successfully several times in the past, and her advocate was confident this, too, would be a positive experience.

We talked on the phone several times with the woman chaperone *(I'll call her "Glenda")* who would escort Becky. In addition, we'd mailed her the written information concerning medication, spending money, how to reach us for emergencies, and all other usual instructions and permissions parents or guardians are routinely required to provide.

The first half of the trip went well. The group had several wonder-filled days at Disneyland.

On the way home, however, Glenda decided to deplane in Portland, contrary to what she'd personally promised us. Since one of the male escorts was going through to Seattle, Becky was placed in his charge. We and Cascade would have nixed the entire trip, of course, had we known this part of the contract would be broken. The agency specifically promised that only females would chaperone females at all times.

When the plane landed in Seattle, according to Cascade's instructions, the escort would direct Becky to an airport shuttle to take her to Bellingham. Arrangements were already in place for a taxicab to meet her there and take her to her apartment in Lynden. In fact, the fares for the shuttle and cab were included in the package fee charged by the travel agency.

Instead, the male escort deplaning with her said, "I'm outa here. I gotta go meet my own family. I want to spend some time with them. Good luck, kid," or words to that effect.

When our phone rang shortly after midnight, I jumped to answer it so it wouldn't wake my slumbering husband.

The woman on the other end of the line identified herself as the manager of a snack bar in Sea-Tac Airport. She related what happened when she saw our daughter standing alone nearby, sobbing her heart out.

She went to Becky and asked, "Are you in trouble?"

"Yes. I can't get home. Nobody pick me up," she wailed.

"Shall I call someone for you?"

"Yes, call my dad and mom," Becky said, giving her a slip of paper with our phone number on it.

119

"We will be there as soon as possible, probably 45 minutes or so," I told this kind woman.

After she gave me the door number nearest her concession stand, I asked a favor: "Please have her sit down close by and stay in that one place. We'll find her."

The phone rang again the moment I hung up. It was Lisa Deubler from Cascade. She had heard from the shuttle company that Becky had not boarded the van. The driver had waited for a reasonable time and was now on the way back to Bellingham with the rest of his passengers.

"What in the world could have happened?" Lisa asked.

After explaining what I knew, I asked Lisa, "Will you please cancel Becky's taxi at the airport? And be sure to inform her supervisor tomorrow that she won't be in for work. It will be impossible for us to drive her home tonight. We'll have to drive her home tomorrow."

After I woke Paul, it didn't take much time to get the car on the freeway, but every one of those thirty miles to the airport seemed like ten thousand.

Once there and parked, we determined where "Door 16" was and scurried to the short stairway.

"Mom! Dad!" a familiar voice called.

Becky was at the bottom of the steps facing the stairway, seated near an older man in a wheelchair and his wife.

"Hello!" the woman greeted us warmly. "We've been having a good conversation with Becky."

She introduced herself as a former eighth grade teacher and said, "When the snack bar manager told her to sit down until her parents came, my husband and I realized

Becky was in some kind of trouble. We decided to stay with her until you got here."

"Oh, thank you!" Paul exclaimed.

The former teacher continued, "Becky asked where a bathroom was, and I took her to one instead of just giving her directions. I know how easily confused one can get in this huge place."

At that point, a fortyish-looking lady sitting on the end of the row spoke up.

"I'm also a teacher, and I was watching your daughter, too. I made up my mind I wouldn't leave here either, until I knew she was with her parents."

Guardian angels couldn't have looked any better than these people!

After I nagged the negligent travel service by mail and telephone for several weeks, the manager finally sent Becky a check to reimburse her for the unused shuttle ticket and cab.

Cascade also attempted, but failed to get, reimbursement for the day's wages Becky missed, and payment for our mileage to and from Sea-Tac, and for driving to Lynden and back the next day. Needless to say, that agency is now on the "blacklist" of service providers for Cascade clientele.

Trips, Inc., the special travel agency Becky and other Cascade residents now use exclusively has proven to be completely trustworthy.

In one of her earlier-than-I'd-like "Hey, Mom!" calls this spring, she asked, "You care if I go to Scotland?"

"No, Becky, I don't care," I said. "That will be exciting!"

"Really? I can go?"

"Do you have enough money, Becky?"

"Oh, I got a whole *lotsa* money!" she answered.

Yes, Becky plans to go to Scotland with a Trips, Inc. tour this fall, but she really doesn't have a "whole lot" of money. Each time she decides where she will spend her vacation, she puts a small amount aside each month toward it. The down payment is usually the whole sum of her savings. Then she makes a monthly payment toward it. Like the other trips she's taken, the one to Scotland will be completely paid for by the time she leaves. Her passport is safely in Cascade's possession.

Great changes in educational training and laws over the past number of years have enabled our "little bird" to fly away from our nest and find her own niche in life. Perceptions of what a mentally challenged person is able and allowed to do have been dramatic. But we are convinced all that has happened for Becky's good isn't just because of policies and laws against discrimination enacted by the government. We see these more as an opus composed and orchestrated by our Father God alone.

With such a director, how could anyone in our house sing any sad songs!

Our New Niche

I love you, Becky,
For who you are now--
Warm, loving daughter,
My special parcel
Gift-wrapped by God.

I look beyond Now,
Awed to see you change
When our Jesus comes:
Truly whole, redeemed,
Formed new in Him.

I too shall change, when
Before His bright throne,
Loosed from sin's steel chains
Shackling us to Earth,
We'll dance with Grace;

We'll sip sweet, sweet wine
Of Jesus' pure love,
Swing on Heaven's Gate,
Skip silver pebbles
On Golden Shores.

Redeemed! Made complete!
His clear Light shall shine
Through us: bright diamonds
In His crown, rainbows
Shaped by His tears!

DON'T SING ANY SAD SONGS

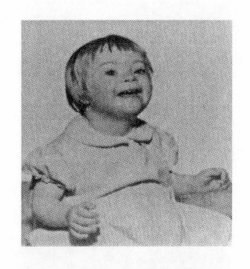

DEAR MOM   2/28/97
I LOVE MY JOB,
LearNing NEW thinGS
CLeaNing   Listening To boss

WE HaVe A staff Party
With PIZZA aT NiGht And
PoP At MY PLace. My RooMate
Franes, EVELyN, Dave, SuSan,
Karin Tanya, and Martin
and George   3/4/97

tomorrow IS shopping
I think I have A choice on weight
Wotches and ReguLAR Dinner
Swanson. I Like chicken, I Like
hamberger I Like French Fres.

        I Love you
          Becky Icenhower

127

DON'T SING ANY SAD SONGS

Chapter 16
Let's Talk About Disabilities

This section is designed to facilitate discussion among parents, teachers, Sunday School workers, or caregivers involved with special needs children or adults. Pastors and others wanting an insight into spiritual dynamics of families of mentally/physically challenged children also will benefit from these exercises.

Discussion I - Denial, Blame, Frustration, Anger

1. Read Ephesians 2:1-10, 2:14-18; James 1:19-21.
2. Discuss this statement in light of the scriptures you've just read: "Denial, blame, frustration, and anger are common parental reactions when a child with mental or physical disabilities is born to them."
3. Role play a scene between a mother and father just learning their newborn has one or more of these challenges:
    a. congenital deformities
    b. Down syndrome
    c. blindness
4. Parental drug abuse or sexually transmitted disease bring natural consequences to offspring:
    a. Such irresponsible parental behavior cannot and should not be forgiven by God or His people.
    b. I don't want my kids around the boy next door who's disabled because his father had a sexually transmitted disease. After all, my kids might "catch" it from drinking from a cup he's touched.

5. Hostility toward a "flawed" child is sinful. However, hateful attitudes toward ancestors who passed along genetic flaws are justified.

Discussion II - Socialization, Laughter, and Fun

1. Read Psalm 4:6-7; Psalm 5:11-12; Nehemiah 8:10 - "Do not grieve, for the joy of the Lord is your strength."

2. These statements are actual quotations. Tell why you agree or disagree with them:

a. "Mentally handicapped people are always happy. They cannot experience grief or depression as other people do."

b. "There is no essential difference between laughing *with* and laughing *at* a person with disabilities."

c. "Joy is not a meaningful part of any developmentally delayed individual's life, since they don't understand jokes."

d. "Socialization with people of normal intelligence and abilities is a factor for growth and change for many mentally and physically impaired children and adults."

e. "I don't think that people who are mentally or physically handicapped from birth mature sexually; they do not have sexual feelings or desires."

f. "Well, o.k., so mentally and physically challenged people *do* have romantic feelings. I still don't think they should be able to get married like 'regular' people. Maybe it's o.k. for them just to live together, because they can't have babies anyway."

g. "I'm embarrassed to be seen with Alan; people may think he's my brother, or something."

130

3. Think of four activities or hobbies you can share (and truly enjoy) with special needs children and adults. What would you do if your 25-year-old mentally challenged friend's only hobby is coloring in a color book? Would you be willing to teach that person another skill, for variety's sake?

Discussion III - Spiritual Life

1. Read I Thessalonians 5:14, 16-18; Luke 18:15-18
2. How would you answer these statements?
a. "There is *always* a connection between illnesses, mental and physical handicaps and unconfessed sin or not trusting God. For this reason, the parents have only themselves to blame for their children's disabilties."
b. "My aunt's cousin Julie took her crippled son to a tent revival where the evangelist prayed for the boy. He was healed and is now completed normal. Maybe you should trust God for *your* child's healing!"
c. "My granddaughter, who has Down syndrome, prayed and asked Jesus into her heart. Our son thinks she shouldn't give her testimony in church or ask to be baptized, because she might not understand what the Bible says. What do you think?"
d. "We shouldn't worry about the salvation of people who were born with disabilities, because they are really angels in disguise."

Discussion IV: Church and Community Social Life

1. Read Ephesians 4:4-7; 4-32a.

2. Name four ways you can help integrate people with special needs into your church's social activities and community activities.

3. Would you be comfortable pairing up in a "buddy system" with a disabled young person or adult? This would involve a variety of activities outside of a church setting. Suggestions: going to an acceptable movie of his or her choice, eating lunch or dinner together, spending a day at an amusement park or fair, swimming, going to a ballgame. What problems do you anticipate, and how could these be solved?

4. What kind of guidelines should be in place before you begin your "buddy" relationship? How can you make sure your "buddy" understands this relationship *(for instance, if he/she insists upon an inappropriate display of affection or does not want to spend his/her own money that has been budgeted for an event, but expects you to pay for everything)?*

5. What can you do to solve the problem of monopolization of your time by your friend? How often may he/she call you? What is a "reasonable" time to spend together *(in terms of hours)?*

6. What kind of relationship should you form with your buddy's parent, guardian, or advocate?

7. If after a time, you find the relationship is not mutually comfortable, what should you do? *(Remember, many mentally handicapped adults can be very sensitive about perceived rejection.)*

Chapter 17
Where to Find Assistance

Birth parents and adoptive couples are sometimes bewildered, uncertain about what their new baby's physical or mental impairment entails.

"Where do we turn for assistance?" is one of the first questions they ask. "We really want to contact somebody or some place, where we may turn for help. We want our child to come to his full potential, with God's help."

Fifty years ago, parents were told to "Just take her home and love her. There isn't anything that can be done." In some extreme cases, that is still true, but now much is happening with medical research and training programs. Today's parents can expect more help *(and sensitivity)* from various agencies and medical personnel.

Your pediatrician, of course, will be the first to offer you pamphlets about developmental and physical growth benchmarks, and provide valuable guidance about eating, sleeping, and medical problems. Pediatricians also play strong, supportive roles in directing you to others providing significant help.

Other than for our first pediatrician who asked if we wanted our daughter to have medical treatment, Becky always has had kind and attentive medical and dental caregivers, for which we are profoundly grateful.

Believe me, you'll also have numerous well-intentioned friends, acquaintances, and even a few strangers, who will give you a ton of unwanted, unsolicited, unscientific advice and "secret" prescriptions. You'll be told that a certain "cure" is available in Mexico or Argentina or Europe; or a particular unregulated drug,

Chinese herb, or a mega-vitamin regimen is what your child needs. Supposedly, the American Medical Association and the Federal Drug Administration "don't want you to know" about some of these.

Desperate parents can be targeted by charlatans who see them as "cash cows." There are no "magic cures" from gypsies or psychics. When these opportunists take advantage of the situation, the children lose ground while their parents' pockets are being picked.

Once in a great while a particular doctor or dentist will not want to accept a physically or mentally challenged child as a patient, or shows hostility in some way. One mother told me of a doctor who was concerned that his upscale clientele would be "offended" by her son's bizarre condition. That is discriminatory -- and rare. Personally, I wouldn't "push" such a doctor into accepting my child as a patient. Ask for a referral from the local American Medical Association chapter to find another professional if there is rudeness, coldness, or obvious lack of concern. If you are new in town, it is likely that other parents with handicapped children can recommend doctors and dentists they use.

Universities and teaching hospitals are taking leadership in the areas of disability sensitivity, so there is far less blatant discrimination these days. Far more pediatricians, family practice doctors, hospitals and birthing centers are guiding parents to training and educational facilities. Most nurses and office personnel are well-informed and genuinely interested in seeing that parents know what services are available.

Unfortunately, some church and Sunday School volunteers, do not always have the knowledge or expertise to direct or help with handicapped children's spiritual training. This is especially true in small, independent churches, or in rural or semi-isolated communities. However, more and more church denominations publish religious materials specifically written or adapted for the deaf, blind, physically or mentally challenged. Contact your church leadership or denominational headquarters for information. Your local Christian bookstore personnel can special order appropriate materials to use at home as well.

Here is a list of other resources available for families, communities, and churches. Certainly it is not intended to be comprehensive, but it is a place to start. One group or person may lead you to a new group or organization based in your own community.

TOYS

1. **Dolly Downs** is a doll having Down's syndrome features. It is available in boy or girl versions, with a choice of ethnic skin and hair color. It is manufactured in a sheltered workshop by developmentally delayed adults: To order, write:

Camp Venture, Inc.
100 Covenant Road
PO Box 402
Nanuet, NY 10954

or phone: 1(800) 682-3714 for current cost. Payment may be made by check, money order, VISA or Master Card. *(Residents of New York also pay state tax.)*

2. **Lekotek Toy Resource Hotline** provides help in selecting toys and other play materials for children with disabilities. Toll-free assistance is available Monday through Friday, 9:00-4:00 CST Phone: 1(800)366-7529.

3. **Lekotek** *(see above)*, along with the National Parent Network on Disabilities and the Toys 'R Us chain, co-publishes "Toy Guide for Differently Abled Kids!" The guide is available at all U.S. Toys 'R Us stores, or by mail from:

Toys 'R Us Toy Guide
461 From Road
Paramus, NJ 07652

BIBLE STUDIES

1. Friendship Bible Studies *(U.S. only)*:

The Friendship Foundation
2850 Kalamazoo Avenue
Grand Rapids, MI 49560
Phone: 1(800)333-8300

2. Friendship Bible Studies *(Canada only)*:

The Friendship Foundation
P.O.Box 5070
Burlington, ON, Canada, L7R348
Phone: 1(800)263-4252

SPECIAL TRAVEL

TRIPS, Inc.
Special Adventures
1901 Fairmount Blvd.
Eugene, OR 97403
Phone: 1(800)686-1013

TRIPS, Inc. has this written mission statement:

"To provide travel opportunities to people of various abilities in a safe, respectful, and fun atmosphere. All of our special adventures seek to create an environment that promotes personal and emotional growth, friendship, and learning."

The planned trips, departing from Portland, OR, or Seattle, WA, are specifically designed for those with developmental disabilities and other disabilities requiring assistance. *(Arrangements can be made for others outside these areas to join the group in Portland, en route, or at final destination.)* They accommodate those in wheelchairs, including those who require their own chaperones for safety. Travelers have 24-hour professional supervision *(staff-to-traveler is one-to-four),* assistance with medications, and budgeting their souvenir money so it doesn't run out the first day. Female travelers always have female chaperones.

Jim Peterson, executive director of TRIPS, Inc., has a masters degree in Special Education and has worked in the field for 17 years.

LITERATURE AND NEWSLETTERS

1. Joni Eareckson Tada, widely known throughout the world for her inspirational testimony at Billy Graham Crusades, is a popular writer and advocate for those who by accident or by birth need specialized training. She herself became a quadriplegic as a teenager after a diving accident. She produces beautiful mouth-paintings, some of which are featured on greeting cards and Christmas cards. Her ministry organization can be reached through this address:

Joni and Friends
P. O. Box 3333
Agoura Hills, CA 91376-3333

2. Another excellent newsletter, *The Matchmaker*, provides connections for parents of children with disorders, disabilities, or chromosomal abnormalities. From a database of over 9,000 families covering more than 1,600 disorders, very rare syndromes or conditions can be matched. Parents then can exchange valuable medical information, as well as the names of doctors, clinics, and medical resources or research programs. Families provide one another with emotional support, so they don't have to feel alone. To subscribe ($10.00 a year) write to:

The Matchmaker
MUMS
National Parent-to-Parent Network Newsletter
Julie Gordon
150 Custer Court
Green Bay, WI 54301

Phone: (414)336-5333.

3. For a Disabilities Resource List with information on a wide variety of books, tapes, booklets, etc., write to:

Focus on the Family
Correspondence Department
Colorado Springs, CO 80995

4. For a free newsletter, *Point of Departure*, focusing on rehabilitation and employment projects relating to transition services for students with disabilities, contact:

TATRA Project
c/o PACER Center
4826 Chicago Avenue S.
Minneapolis, MN 55417
Phone: (612)827-2966 or
e-mail: mnpacer@edu.gte.net

Point of Departure also includes articles on parent advocacy, job interviews, transition planning, and outcome evaluation.

5. Public libraries can assist you in locating periodical literature, research materials, and videos. Watch also for public information programs sponsored by Friends of the Library or others at your local or county library.

OTHER SERVICES

1. The Veterans Administration may determine eligibility for financial and medical assistance for a handicapped son or daughter, if a parent has been honorably discharged with a permanent, service-connected disability. *(Under normal circumstances, no aid goes to children after they reach 18, but if the handicapping condition began before 18, is continuing or permanent, support is extended after certain procedures are followed.)*

2. Be sure to check with Social Security Administration for Supplemental Security Income (SSI). SSI is a public assistance program for children and adults who are blind or disabled or have limited income or resources. *(The applicant may have some income and still qualify for SSI.)* For more information about Social Security and Supplemental Security Income eligibility rules, contact the Social Services Administration toll-free at 1-800-772-1213. Ask for a copy of these booklets: *Social Security: Understanding the Benefits* (SSA Pub.No.05-10024) and *Supplemental Security Income* (SSA Pub.No.05-11000). If you have Internet use, go to www.ssa.gov to access these and other publications.

3. Contact your local Department of Social and Health Services (DSHS) for a variety of services, including financial eligibility for skill training leading to employment.

4. Local public school districts, community colleges, or universities may be able to test, refer to others, or offer

specialized or adapted training for differently abled children and adults.

5. Local chapters of Association for Retarded Citizens are generally listed in the telephone directory under A R C of -- County. The phone number in the Seattle (King County) area is (206)364-4645. If there is no local address or phone for A R C in your area, the national headquarters address is:

National A R C
P. O. Box 6109,
2709 Avenue E East
Arlington, TX 76011

6. Nearly every hamlet, village and urban area has a Special Olympics program, though you may have to look hard to find one in your local phone book. Your school district office, sheltered workshop, or group home should be able to help you. Special Olympians bowl, run, swim, bike, jump, play basketball, lift weights -- in short, nearly every sports activity that "regular" Olympians do. Best of all, everyone is a winner! A wonderful boost to self-esteem, morale, and physical fitness!

7. Many local YMCAs, Boy Scouts, Girl Scouts, Campfire Girls, etc. have adapted programs suitable for physically or mentally challenged children and adults. Easter Seals often sponsor day camps.

8. Seek information from your local Lions Club, Shriners, Muscular Dystrophy, Cerebral Palsy or other

service organizations with a particular interest in serving those with special problems.

9. Sheltered workshops, group homes, and other similar organizations may be listed in telephone directories under "Disabled Services" or "Disabled Persons Assistance Services."

10. Many city buses have wheelchair lifts. Some bus companies, usually funded through city or county agencies, provide special van transportation for disabled persons of any age for doctor appointments, grocery shopping, etc. The cost per ride is extremely reasonable.

11. If you have a computer with Internet connection, perhaps you've already discovered this helpful site: The *Seattle Times* (p. E2, February12, 1997) says this is "THE Web site for information related to special needs kids:"

http://www.familyvillage.wisc.edu/tindex.htm

See the next chapter for recommended books and bookstore web sites.

Chapter 18
Books and Bookstore Web Sites

Searching on the World Wide Web brings up many intriguing book titles under "Down syndrome" and other mental and physical handicaps. Titles, authors, publication dates, and prices are listed. Most of the listings, in hard cover or paperback, may be purchased on-line. *(You'll want to click the option "Read more about this title" before you do that, for titles can be quite deceptive.)* You'll find hundreds of them after the initial search. There are textbooks for professionals or college courses, fiction for children and young adults; other family-oriented stories, both fiction and non-fiction.

Look also for good used books in your local Friends of the Library sales of donated books and in second hand bookstores in your own neighborhood. Some are treasures!

Here is a list of some web sites (URLs) you may wish to browse. Other sites may be found in the Yellow Pages of your local phone book. More are being added regularly.

Amazon - http://www.amazon.com
Barnes & Noble - http://www.barnesandnoble.com
Book Stacks Unlimited - http://www.books.com
Books On Line -
http://www.c.s.cmu.edu/web/booktitles.html
Bookport - http://www.bookport.com/welcome/9550
Bookwire - http://www.bookwire.com
BookZone - http://www.bookzone.com
Borders Book Store - http://www.borders.com

Christian Resource Outlet - http://www.crobookstore.com
The American Book Center - http://www.abc.ni

My own first and foremost recommendation for a
comprehensive book is *Extraordinary Kids*, by Cheri
Fuller, et al. It is a best seller published by Focus on the
Family in 1997, and winner of the Gold Medallion Award
at the 1998 Christian Booksellers Association. This book,
discussing many aspects of disabilities and special
education, is wholeheartedly endorsed by educators, church
personnel, and parents.

Since *Don't Sing Any Sad Songs* is not a textbook nor
a "how-to" book, I asked the Rev. Jim Vanderlaan, director
of Disability Concerns and editor of "Breaking Barriers,"
for the past fifteen years, to share some of his
knowledgeable recommendations. Look for them in local
bookstores, public libraries, or urge your church library to
purchase some of them:

An Ark for the Poor: The Story of L'Arche, Jean Vanier.
Novalis Publishing (in Canada), Crossroad (in U.S.) 1995,
125 pages. $10.95
A brief but moving story of L'Arche's first 30 years.
Written by the founder of these communities where
disabled and abled live together. Today over 115 homes
are found in 125 countries. Not a date-and-place account so
much as a history demonstrating that the kingdom is among
us and that, as our Lord said, it can be found among the
weak and poor. Challenges notions about people with
mental impairments.

A Committed Mercy: You and Your Church Can Serve the Disabled, Stan Carder. Baker, 1995, 128 pages. $10.99
"Where do we begin? How do we begin a ministry for people with disabilities in our church?" Ever heard or asked these questions? Read Carder. From the biblical grounds (imagebearers) to learning theory; from your discomfort with "them" to hard truths about what goes on inside their families. Good training manual *(chapters end with discussion questions)* for small group study and for churches beginning a ministry.

Emmaus Eyes: Worship with the Mentally Challenged, Lo-Ann and David Trembley. Eden, 1996. 87 pages. $14.95
The Tremblys are co-pastors to a congregation with a large number of mentally impaired members. Do people understand the gospel? Do we need new ways to communicate that gospel without compromising it? We learn how to do that, they argue, only when our congregation is inclusive. We know that the people able to teach us the most are those most different from us. Yet we persist in assembling in homogeneous congregations. The authors give us portraits and stories of a diverse body. And they beg us to not let our sense of the presence of God get lost in our style of worship.

Flowers from the Ark: True Stories from the Homes of L'Arche, Christella Buser. Paulist Press, 1996, 104 pages. $7.95
Buser gathered stories *(most are only a few lines long)* from the homes of L'Arche -- a network of homes for adults with developmental disabilities. These stories are often witty, but always full of insight and wisdom. A must-read for

those who think the Kingdom can function perfectly well without the mentally impaired.

From Barriers to Bridges: A Community Action Guide for Congregations and People with Disabilities, Ginny Thornburgh (ed). National Organization on Disability, 1996. 62 pages. $10.00
A manual designed to aid dialogue between people with disabilities, their families, religious institutions, and the community. Includes all necessary planning ingredients plus details from eight church/community conferences.

From the Heart: On Being the Mother of a Child with a Disability, Jane March and Carol Boggis (eds), Woodbine House, 1996. 225 pages. $14.95
Nine moms tell their stories. *(How else can you and I learn what it's like?)* A wide range of disabilities.

Guide My Feet: Prayers and Meditations for Our Children, Marian Wright Edelman. Harper Perennial, 1995. 208 pages. $10.00
The founder and president of the Children's Defense Fund was prompted to write these prayers because her "heart breaks watching fragile little humans struggle for life." She is referring to infants with and without disabilities and to young children and teens in a world "in which Herod seems to rule." Edelman taught me to be a better pray-er. For parents, grandparents, and all others who care that children across this globe are threatened. And for those who know that our Lord uses children to instruct us concerning his kingdom.

146

Psalms of Lament, Ann Weems. Westminster John Knox, 1995. 104 pages. $12.00
Fifty psalms that assail heaven with "why" prayers. Unlike many such attempts, Weems' psalms contain the ingredients of biblical psalms: awe, grievance, petition, vengeance, rejoicing. The laments are many: death of a loved one *(Weems lost a 21-year-old son)*, a child gone astray, a disability, friends who hurt us. Her first psalm contains the line: "hosannas stuck in my throat." Do you know the feeling? Perhaps the best book of its class in quite a few years.

Religion and Disability: Essays in Scripture, Theology and Ethics, Marilyn Bishop (ed). Sheed and Ward, 1995. 64 pages. $6.95
Three essays (by an Anglican, a Roman Catholic, and a Methodist) from a recent conference sponsored by the National Council of Churches' Committee on Disabilities. The three are entitled: "Beware of the Canaanite Woman: Disability and the Bible," by Donald Senior; "Theological Reflections on Disability," by John Macquarrie; and "The Church and Handicapped Persons: A Continuing Challenge to the Imagination," by Stanley Hauerwas. This work is far more inspiring than the titles might suggest. The reader will work a little, but not too much. In any case, the effort will be rewarded.

Uncommon Fathers: Reflections on Raising a Child with a Disability, Donald Meyer (ed). Woodbine House, 1996. 224 pages. $14.95
A companion volume to *From the Hear*. The plea of these dads is simple: walk with us; see with our eyes; listen with

147

and to us; learn with us how much these sons and daughters are needed in our communities -- including our faith communities.

When It Hurts to Live: Devotions for Difficult Times, Kathleen Kern. Faith and Life Press, 1995. 208 pages. $11.95
Forty devotions by the writer of a Bible study curriculum for adults. Depression is the focus *(the author has experienced three episodes of depression)* and each devotion follows a uniform format adaptable for group study: a lengthy Scripture passage quoted, analysis of the passage, application, questions, and prayer. A balanced view of depression.

CHILDREN'S BOOKS

Are There Stripes in Heaven?, Lee Klein. Paulist Press, 1994. Unpaged. $4.95
Patrick's bad Sunday turns out good when he begins to see things through his sister's eyes. Colleen, his sister, has Down's syndrome. Ages 2-6

Listen for the Bus: David's Story, Patricia McMahon. Boyds Mills Press, 1995. 48 pages. $15.95
A book of story and photos, and both will stir the imagination. David is off to kindergarten. David is blind. His classmates now get to find out how David has learned to eat, play, travel, read, curl up in Mom's lap -- in other words, to live. Seventy-five photos of David accompany the text. Ages 2-6

Marrying Malcolm Murgatroyd, Mame Farrell. Farrar, Strauss, Giroux, 1995. 122 pages. $14.00.
Hannah likes friend and neighbor Malcolm. He is a slow learner, and none of the names he is called are pleasant ones. Hannah defends him, extricates him from mean pranks, and fears the ridicule she'll get for doing so. Malcolm befriends her brother Ian, who has muscular dystrophy and uses a wheel chair. Ages 6-10

A Very Special Critter (in the Little Critter series), Gina and Mercer Meyer. Golden Books, 1992. Unpaged. $3.95
Alex gets included in the classroom even though he's in a wheel chair. By the end of the story everyone is convinced he is just one of the gang. Ages 2-5

DON'T SING ANY SAD SONGS

ROSALIE B. ICENHOWER

My Special Child

I never would have chosen you,
O child of mine, little bird
With broken wing.
I'd have chosen a brighter bird
Who could rise on wings of praise
To sing to God.

But God, in His infinite care,
Chose you for me, little girl,
To strengthen me.
You have taught me greater love:
My heart is a richer place
Because you came.

I never would have chosen you,
But our God has chosen me
To care for you.
I'd have chosen a perfect child--
And I'd never have known the joy
You've brought to me.

Printed in the United States
5741